EXPLORING THE DEPTHS OF LIFE AND LOVE

A Study of Job, Ecclesiastes, and the
Song of Solomon

Jack W. Hayford
with
Larry R. McQueen

THOMAS NELSON PUBLISHERS
Nashville

Exploring the Depths of Life and Love
Copyright © 1997 by Jack W. Hayford

Published in Nashville, Tennessee, by Thomas Nelson, Inc.

Unless otherwise indicated, Scripture quotations are from the
New King James Version of the Bible, © 1979, 1980, 1982,
Thomas Nelson, Inc., Publishers

Printed in the United States of America
1 2 3 4 5 6 7 8 — 02 01 00 99 98

CONTENTS

· ·

Exploring the Depths of Life and Love is one of a series of study guides that focus exciting, discovery-geared coverage of Bible book and power themes—all prompting toward dynamic, Holy Spirit-filled living.

About the Executive Editor

JACK W. HAYFORD, noted pastor, teacher, writer, and composer, is the Executive Editor of the complete series, working with the publisher in conceiving and developing each of the books.

Dr. Hayford is Senior Pastor of The Church On The Way, the First Foursquare Church of Van Nuys, California. He and his wife, Anna, have four married children, all of whom are active in either pastoral ministry or vital church life. As General Editor of the *Spirit-Filled Life*® *Bible,* Pastor Hayford led a four-year project which has resulted in the availability of one of today's most practical and popular study Bibles. He is author of more than twenty books, including *A Passion for Fullness, The Beauty of Spiritual Language, Rebuilding the Real You,* and *Prayer Is Invading the Impossible.* His musical compositions number over four hundred songs, including the widely sung "Majesty."

About the Writer

LARRY McQUEEN has worked in Christian ministry for more than ten years. After serving as interim pastor at his home church in Texas, he completed a master's program and began teaching part-time in the Bible and Christian ministries department at Lee University in Cleveland, Tennessee. He currently works as an archivist at the Hal Bernard Dixon Jr. Pentecostal Research Center in Cleveland, Tennessee, and serves his local congregation as church administrator.

Larry earned a B.A. in biblical education at Lee University, an M.Div. at the Church of God Theological Seminary, and a Th.M. from Columbia Theological Seminary in Decatur, Georgia. His writing includes material published by Sheffield Academic Press, Sheffield, England.

THE GIFT
THAT KEEPS ON GIVING

Who doesn't like presents? Whether they come wrapped in colorful paper and beautiful bows, or brown paper bags closed and tied at the top with old shoestring. Kids and adults of all ages love getting and opening presents.

But even this moment of surprise and pleasure can be marked by dread and fear. All it takes is for these words to appear: "Assembly Required. Instructions Enclosed." How we hate these words! They taunt us, tease us, beckon us to try to challenge them, all the while knowing that they have the upper hand. If we don't understand the instructions, or if we ignore them and try to put the gift together ourselves, more than likely, we'll only assemble frustration and anger. What we felt about our great gift—all the joy, anticipation, and wonder—will vanish. And they will never return, at least not to that pristine state they had before we realized that *we* had to assemble our present with instructions *no consumer* will ever understand.

One of the most precious gifts God has given us is His Word, the Bible. Wrapped in the glory and sacrifice of His Son and delivered by the power and ministry of His Spirit, it is a treasured gift—one the family of God has preserved and protected for centuries as a family heirloom. It promises that it is the gift that keeps on giving, because the Giver it reveals is inexhaustible in His love and grace.

Tragically, though, fewer and fewer people, even those who number themselves among God's everlasting family, are opening this gift and seeking to understand what it's all about and how to use it. They often feel intimidated by it. It requires some assembly, and its instructions are hard to comprehend sometimes. How does the Bible fit together anyway? What does

Genesis have to do with Revelation? Who are Abraham and Moses, and what is their relationship to Jesus and Paul? And what about the works of the Law and the works of faith? What are they all about, and how do they fit together, if at all?

And what does this ancient Book have to say to us who are looking toward the twenty-first century? Will taking the time and energy to understand its instructions and to fit it all together really help you and me? Will it help us better understand who we are, what the future holds, how we can better live here and now? Will it really help us in our personal relationships, in our marriages and families, in our jobs? Can it give us more than just advice on how to handle crises? the death of a loved one? the financial fallout of losing a job? catastrophic illness? betrayal by a friend? the seduction of our values? the abuses of the heart and soul? Will it allay our fears and calm our restlessness and heal our wounds? Can it really get us in touch with the same power that gave birth to the universe? that parted the Red Sea? that raised Jesus from the stranglehold of the grave? Can we really find unconditional love, total forgiveness, and genuine healing in its pages?

Yes. Yes. Without a shred of doubt.

The *Spirit-Filled Life® Bible Discovery Guide* series is designed to help you unwrap, assemble, and enjoy all God has for you in the pages of Scripture. It will focus your time and energy on the books of the Bible, the people and places they describe, and the themes and life applications that flow thick from its pages like honey oozing from a beehive.

So you can get the most out of God's Word, this series has a number of helpful features. Each study guide has no more than fourteen lessons, each arranged so you can plumb the depths or skim the surface, depending on your needs and interests.

The study guides also contain six major sections, each marked by a symbol and heading for easy identification.

WORD WEALTH

The WORD WEALTH feature provides important definitions of key terms.

BEHIND THE SCENES

BEHIND THE SCENES supplies information about cultural beliefs and practices, doctrinal disputes, business trades, and the like that illuminate Bible passages and teachings.

AT A GLANCE

The AT A GLANCE features uses maps and charts to identify places and simplify themes or positions.

BIBLE EXTRA

Because this study guide focuses on a book of the Bible, you will find a BIBLE EXTRA feature that guides you into the Bible dictionaries, Bible encyclopedias, and other resources that will enable you to glean more from the Bible's wealth if you want something extra.

PROBING THE DEPTHS

Another feature, PROBING THE DEPTHS, will explain controversial issues raised by particular lessons and cite Bible passages and other sources to which you can turn to help you come to your own conclusions.

FAITH ALIVE

Finally, each lesson contains a FAITH ALIVE feature. Here the focus is, So what? Given what the Bible says, what does it mean for my life? How can it impact my day-to-day needs, hurts, relationships, concerns, and whatever else is important to me? FAITH ALIVE will help you see and apply the practical relevance of God's literary gift.

As you'll see, these guides supply space for you to answer the study and life-application questions and exercises. You may, however, want to record all your answers, or just the overflow from your study or application, in a separate notebook or journal. This would be especially helpful if you think you'll dig into the BIBLE EXTRA features. Because the exercises in this feature are optional and can be expanded as far as you want to take them, we have not allowed writing space for them in this study guide. So you may want to have a notebook or journal handy for recording your discoveries while working through this feature's riches.

The Bible study method used in this series revolves around four basic steps: observation, interpretation, correlation, and application. Observation answers the question, What does the text say? Interpretation deals with, What does the text mean?—not with what it means to you or me, but what it meant to its original readers. Correlation asks, What light do other Scripture passages shed on this text? And application, the goal of Bible study, poses the question, How should my life change in response to the Holy Spirit's teaching of this text?

If you have used a Bible much before, you know that it comes in a variety of translations and paraphrases. Although you can use any of them with profit as you work through the *Spirit-Filled Life® Bible Discovery Guide* series, when Bible passages or words are cited, you will find they are from the New King James Version of the Bible. Using this translation with this series will make your study easier, but it's certainly not necessary.

The only resources you need to complete and apply these study guides are a heart and mind open to the Holy Spirit, a prayerful attitude, and a pencil and a Bible. Of course, you may draw upon other sources, such as commentaries, dictionaries, encyclopedias, atlases, and concordances, and you'll even find some optional exercises that will guide you into these sources. But these are extras, not necessities. These study guides are comprehensive enough to give you all you need to gain a good, basic understanding of the Bible book being covered and how you can apply its themes and counsel to your life.

A word of warning, though. By itself, Bible study will not transform your life. It will not give you power, peace, joy, comfort, hope, and a number of other gifts God longs for you to unwrap and enjoy. Through Bible study, you will grow in your understanding of the Lord, His kingdom and your place in it, but you must be sure to rely on the Holy Spirit to guide your study and your application of the Bible's truths. He, Jesus promised, was sent to teach us "all things" (John 14:26; cf. 1 Cor. 2:13). So as you use this series to guide you through Scripture, bathe your study time in prayer, asking the Spirit of God to illuminate the text, enlighten your mind, humble your will, and comfort your heart. He will never let you down.

My prayer and goal for you is that as you unwrap and begin to explore God's Book for living His way, the Holy Spirit will fill every fiber of your being with the joy and power God longs to give all His children. So read on. Be diligent. Stay open and submissive to Him. You will not be disappointed. He promises you!

EXPLORING THE DEPTHS OF SUFFERING
(JOB 1—42)

The Book of Job is a story to which everyone can relate. It deals with some haunting questions which most of us keep stored somewhere in the back of our minds until we ourselves are faced with personal suffering. We are all acquainted with loss and pain, yet we make every effort possible to keep it at a distance, both physically and mentally.

Job brings us up close to the questions. Here was an innocent man, honest in his dealings with others, prosperous in material things, loving toward his family, upright in his relationship with God—who experienced extreme loss and pain. The story asks the question "why?" from several perspectives. Job's wife, Job's friends, and Job himself all have preconceived notions which give different twists to the "why" question. From heaven's perspective the question is put more in terms of "who?" and "where?" The Book of Job invites us to explore these questions and hear the answer which God gives.

Lesson 1/Satan's Challenge
Job 1—2

Do you know someone, or perhaps an entire family, who seems to have it all together? Beautiful home, nice cars, picture-perfect kids, great job, excellent reputation—life appears to be perfect for them. Unless we are prone toward jealousy, we applaud them. We think, "That is the way life should be."

Such a lifestyle described the biblical character of Job. He had little about which to complain. His life seemed picture-perfect and rightly so, for Job was blessed by God. Yet the story soon makes a turn into the valley of pain and takes Job to the limits of human suffering.

WHO WAS JOB?

Although some have suggested that the Book of Job should be taken merely as a parable or illustration, the Bible attests to Job's existence as a real person. The introduction to the story of Job tells us several things about him. List your observations about Job's character and life from the following verses:

Job 1:1

Job 1:2

Job 1:3

Job 1:5

Job is also mentioned in two texts outside the Book of Job. What can be learned about the person of Job from the following references?

Ezekiel 14:14, 20

James 5:11

BEHIND THE SCENES

Scripture itself attests that Job was a real person. Job was a Gentile, thought to have been a descendant of Nahor, Abraham's brother, and knew God by the name of "Shaddai"—The Almighty. There are thirty reference to Shaddai in the Book of Job. Job was a wealthy man living a semi-nomadic lifestyle.[1]

BEHIND THE SCENES

Job was from the land of Uz. Scholars are not agreed on the exact location of Uz. Some associate it with Edom (see Jer. 25:20, 21), while others locate it northeast of Palestine in Hauran (see Gen. 10:23). The indefinite location of the story may be intended to help provide the distance a reader needs to handle the emotional intensity of the difficult subject of suffering.[2] That Job was from outside Palestine also adds to the universal appeal of the story.

BEHIND THE SCENES

The manners, customs, and general lifestyle of Job are from the patriarchal period (about 2000–1800 B.C.). Scholars differ, however, on when it was compiled, as its writing was an obvious recording of a long-standing oral tradition. Those who attribute it to Moses opt for a fifteenth century B.C. date.

Others opt for as late as the second century B.C. Most conservatives assign it to the Solomonic era, the mid-tenth century.[3]

How is Job's family described in terms of:

affluence?

closeness?

Why was Job concerned about his sons? (Job 1:5)

What connection does Job's concern for his sons have to the temptation presented to Job later in the story? (See Job 1:11; 2:9; 3:1.)

If you are a parent, how do you relate to Job's concern for his children expressed in Job 1:5?

 WORD WEALTH

Sons (Job 1:5) is not limited to the meaning "sons," but can also refer to "children" or "descendants" of both genders. A common example is the phrase *b'nay yisrael* (literally, "sons of Israel"), usually translated "children of Israel." The meaning "to build up" or "to fortify" stands behind the root from which "son" is derived. The idea is that a "son" is a builder of future generations.[4] In this reference, the death of Job's sons meant the end of his future.

Job at a Glance[5]

FOCUS	DILEMMA OF JOB	DEBATES OF JOB					DELIVERANCE OF JOB
REFERENCE	1:1 ———— 3:1 ————	15:1 ————	22:1 ————	27:1 ————	32:1 ————	38:1 ————	42:17
DIVISION	CONTROVERSY OF GOD AND SATAN	FIRST CYCLE OF DEBATE	SECOND CYCLE OF DEBATE	THIRD CYCLE OF DEBATE	FINAL DEFENSE OF JOB	SOLUTION OF ELIHU	CONTROVERSY OF GOD WITH JOB
TOPIC	CONFLICT PROSE	DEBATE POETRY					REPENTANCE PROSE
LOCATION	LAND OF UZ (NORTH ARABIA)						
TIME	PATRIARCHAL PERIOD (c. 2000 B.C.)						

THE ATTACK OF SATAN

Job's experience of loss was not by chance or "bad luck." Satan was behind it. The scene in heaven is a reflection of an earthly king's court in ancient times on the day the king's subjects presented themselves for judgment. The royal court included an "adversary" who acted much like an attorney acts today—bringing the faults of the king's subjects to his attention.

In this story, the heavenly "adversary" points out the unfair advantage of God's protection around Job and challenges God to remove it. Then God would see what sort of person Job really was. God consents, not because He wants Job to suffer, but because God has faith in His servant to remain faithful to Him.

Respond to the following statement: The Book of Job is as much about the character of a person's relationship to God as it is about the problem of human suffering.

 WORD WEALTH

Satan (Job 1:6), *satan* (sah-*tahn*); Strong's #7854; An opponent, or the Opponent; the hater; the accuser; adversary, enemy; one who resists, obstructs, and hinders whatever is good. Satan comes from the verb which means "to be an opponent," or "to withstand." As a noun, *satan* can describe any "opponent" (2 Sam. 19:21, 22). However, when the form *ha-satan* (the Adversary) occurs, the translation is usually "Satan," not his name, but his accurate description: hateful enemy. Since Satan is the Hater, he is all the more opposed to God, who is love (see 1 John 3:10–15; 4:7, 8). Humankind did not witness Satan's beginning, but by God's design shall see his end, one of ceaseless torment and humiliation (see Is. 14:12–20; Ezek. 28:16–19; Rev. 20:10).[6]

In the light of Job 1:6–12 and 2:1–7, answer the following questions:

In what way is Satan accountable to God?

What do God's questions for Satan reveal about God's authority?

Is God or Satan behind the evils that curse the earth?

Can Satan do anything of his own accord?

Does Satan have unlimited power to do harm?

How does God describe Job? (1:8; 2:3)

BIBLE EXTRA

The imagery of God's protective "hedge" around Job is also used in other contexts in the Old Testament. Note the similarities and differences in meaning in the following verses:

Psalm 80:12

Isaiah 5:1–7

Psalm 104:5–9

Job 38:8–11

PROBING THE DEPTHS

"Sons of God" (Job 1:6) is the same phrase that occurs in Genesis 6:2. Here, however, its meaning is clearly that of celestial beings or angels God created as His servants. "Satan" is among them. He appears as "the Adversary" to disturb God's kingdom by causing trouble. This is similar to the times when God allowed Satan to influence David to take a census of Israel (1 Chr. 21:1) or when He permitted an evil spirit to torment Saul (1 Sam. 16:14). This is one of only three references where Satan is mentioned by name (see also 1 Chr. 21:1; Zech. 3:1).[7]

List the losses of Job in the first round of Satan's attack:

Job 1:13–15

Job 1:16

Job 1:17

Job 1:18, 19

The celebrations of Job's sons (1:4) probably revolved around their birthdays. The children of Job were killed on the birthday of the "firstborn" (1:18, 19). How does this intensify the calamity? What connection to this theme is found in Job's lament in Job 3?

List the losses of Job in Satan's second round of attack:

2:7

In what ways did the things and people Job lost make up the "hedge" around him?

Name the specific external blessings of God in your life which might constitute your "hedge."

Note the times when it seemed as if your world was crashing down around you. In what ways does Job's story offer new possible explanations of your experience?

BEHIND THE SCENES

Job was stricken with boils (2:7). Other references to this disease include its use as one of the ten plagues God sent upon the Egyptians (Ex. 9:8–12) and as a plague which punishes disobedience to the covenant (Deut. 28:35). It would naturally be taken by Job's friends as a sign of God's wrath upon Job.

What physical afflictions in today's society have been associated with God's judgment?

RESPONSES TO CALAMITY

Humans respond to pain in a variety of ways. Many of the addictions prevalent in society are really attempts to escape suffering. People who do not know God are left only with the attempts at coping with pain.

The story of Job focuses our attention on suffering in the light of our relationship with God. For believers, all aspects of life should be lived out with reference to God. Undeserved suffering is an especially difficult problem precisely because of our relationship with God whom we believe can do anything and who knows everything. Simply coping is not enough. How, then, should believers respond to pain?

Job's initial response included some physical actions (Job 1:20). List these.

How do physical actions help in our response to pain and grief?

In what ways does our society encourage or limit physical actions in our response to extreme loss and grief? How are these healthy or unhealthy?

Job's first response also included a short speech in which he maintains faith in the Lord (Job 1:21, 22). What questions would you ask Job at this point in his story?

It is likely that Job's first response was a conventional confession of someone in grief. What Scriptures or common sayings do you or someone you know recite in times of stress in order to find comfort?

In what ways had Job become "naked"? (v. 21)

In what ways do you identify with Job's initial response to calamity?

Reflect on Job's perspective. The reader of this story knows about the challenge of Satan before the Lord, but apparently Job did not. What, if anything, do you think Job knew about Satan?

Job's second response to calamity was much like his first (1:20, 21). He responded physically (2:8), and he did not "sin with his lips" (2:10). There are, however, subtle changes in the way Job responds. Compare 1:20, 21 and 2:10 and note these changes in terms of:

Statement vs. question

"I" vs. "we"

God's action vs. human reception

What other differences in Job's responses do you notice?

Job's wife challenges Job with a question which remains active throughout the story. It is a question which needed to be asked of Job. It is a question which needs to be asked of us when we face similar experiences: "How long will you hold to your integrity?" How does this question relate to God's comments in Job 2:3?

How does it echo Satan's desire? (Job 2:4, 5)

How does this question open up and reflect the viewpoints of Job's friends in the dialogues? (Job 4—31)

In light of Job's losses and personal suffering, in what does his personal integrity now consist?

If you had been Job's wife, what question would you have asked him?

In the light of your answers to these questions, reflect on times when those closest to you challenged your integrity during difficult times.

How do you respond to the suffering of those closest to you?

 BEHIND THE SCENES

Friends (Job 2:11) is a term used for those showing a solemn, covenant relationship. Job's three friends had a sincere desire to share his grief and ease his pain. Teman was in northern Edom. Shuah was on the Middle Euphrates, below the mouth of the Khabar River. Naamah was between Beirut and Damascus.[8]

Note the reactions of Job's three friends (Job 2:11–13).

List the ways in which Job's friends identify with Job's suffering.

Recall the times you have experienced the shock of seeing a familiar friend or family member whose appearance is altered because of sickness. What emotions did you experience?

These three men "lifted up their voices and wept" (2:12). In ancient near eastern culture, weeping loudly by men was not considered shameful. How does that practice compare to society today?

When is weeping in public acceptable?

How can the church foster occasions and space for both men and women to weep in response to grief?

 FAITH ALIVE

Wise persons live in view of what they know to be true about God, the world, and themselves. Their approach to God is humble and self-effacing, refusing to accuse God of any wrongdoing in adversities. Therefore, the wise are able to patiently embrace and endure suffering, knowing that God's loving hand will prevail beyond it. They know that although we are to seek to live righteously, our righteousness cannot earn God's favor: grace is a gift, not a debt.[9]

FAITH ALIVE

It is God's will that we turn to Him amid our suffering, that we may (a) receive His grace **within** it, and (b) seek His deliverance **from** it. While our individual human responses to pain, difficulty, or tribulation may cause it to become a sanctifying force in our lives, still God has not sanctified suffering.

Jesus' ministry was filled with demonstrations of God removing suffering and releasing people from its agonies. In Christ's ministry we see God's heart: although suffering is a fact, it was not intended as a part of God's order for humanity.[10]

1. *Spirit-Filled Life® Bible* (Nashville: Thomas Nelson Publishers, 1991), 705, "Job: Introduction, Background."

2. J. Gerald Janzen, *Job* (Interpretation Commentary, Atlanta: John Knox Press, 1985), 34, 35.

3. *Spirit-Filled Life® Bible,* 707, "Job: Introduction, Date."

4. Ibid., 49, "Word Wealth: Gen. 29:32, son."

5. *Nelson's Complete Book of Bible Maps and Charts: Old and New Testaments* (Nashville: Thomas Nelson Publishers, 1993), 170.

6. *Spirit-Filled Life® Bible,* 710, "Word Wealth: Job 1:6, Satan."

7. Ibid., note on Job 1:6.

8. Ibid., 712, note on Job 2:11.

9. Ibid., 748–749, "Truth-in-Action through Job."

10. *Hayford's Bible Handbook* (Nashville: Thomas Nelson Publishers, 1995), 128, 131, "Kingdom Key."

Lesson 2/Job's Trust
Job 3—14

"No one ever told me that grief felt so like fear. I am not afraid, but the sensation is like being afraid. The same fluttering in the stomach, the same restlessness, the yawning. I keep on swallowing."[1]

So begins *A Grief Observed,* a published journal which C.S. Lewis wrote after the death of his wife, Joy Davidson. Lewis's journal has comforted thousands of people experiencing grief because it puts into words those feelings which are difficult to express but which long to be expressed, the feelings of utter despair and pain.

The Bible offers several examples of lament which remain within the bounds of the covenant between the speaker and God. One example is Job 3. This opening speech by Job begins a series of dialogues between Job and his three friends who have come to mourn with him.

THE PAIN OF SUFFERING

Up to this point in the story, Job has remained faithful in attitude and speech to God. His words have been pious and well within the acceptable limits of faith. Chapter 3 begins a long series of dialogues which reveal a different attitude, though still not unacceptable. Job opens his soul and reveals his pain in deep lament.

Chapter 3 can be divided into three sections. What are the major themes of each of these sections?

Verses 1–10

Verses 11–19

Verses 20–26

Contrast Job 3:3–5, 26 with the story of creation in Genesis 1:3–5; 2:1–3. How does Job reverse the themes of light, blessing, and rest?

Compare and contrast Job's understanding of the "hedge" of God in Job 3:23 with the "hedge" of God in Job 1:9. How has that which has protected Job now become imprisoning to him?

 WORD WEALTH

male child (Job 3:3), *geber* (*geh*-vehr); Strong's #1397: A champion, hero, warrior, mighty man. In contrast to the other more generic words for man, *geber* refers to a male in all his strength and is derived from *gabar,* "to prevail, have strength."[2] The use of the word here is ironic. When Job should be at the height of his powers as a man, he is instead at his lowest point.

It important to note that Job does not curse God. He does, however, curse the day of his birth (lit. "his day" 3:1). Is Job addressing anyone in particular when speaking this curse?

To whom has Job's attention shifted in this chapter? To God? To his friends? To himself?

Reflect on those times when you wish you did not exist (it's okay to admit). How did your experience compare with Job's?

On whom did your attention focus during those times?

PROBING THE DEPTHS

Do you believe that Job's lament in chapter 3 revealed a lack of faith in God? Or does Job hold onto his integrity through honest confession of deep feelings? Compare Job's lament with the following psalms of lament. What similarities and differences do you see in each?

Psalm 13

Psalm 22

Psalm 88

How do you incorporate lament into your prayers?

What boundaries, if any, do you believe there should be in a believer's honest expression of painful feelings?

FAITH ALIVE

Fear is the converse of faith: it is believing what God says is not true. God commands us not to be afraid. Faith is able to trust God and not act out of fear.

Know and understand that fear shows lack of faith in God and His promises. Rely on the Lord's protection against verbal attacks and do not fear them. Believe that God honors faith that is stronger than death.[3]

CHASTENED BY GOD

Eliphaz is the first of the three friends to speak to Job. This begins a three-cycle dialogue between Job and his friends. Review Job 4—5. What is the basic argument of Eliphaz here?

According to Eliphaz, why do people suffer in the world?

If Eliphaz is correct in his assessment of Job's situation, what should Job do?

PROBING THE DEPTHS

Eliphaz' position is based on the assumption that everyone commits error. He firmly propagates the principle of retribution (4:7–21), noting that God always is compassionate to deliver His children from sorrow (5:9–26). Therefore, Job is being reproved, reaping his own just punishment (4:7). His counsel, however, is wrong.[4]

Compare the instruction Eliphaz received in his "revelation" (4:17–21) with the perspective of Satan in Job 1:9–11. What does this suggest about the "spirit" which Eliphaz saw?

Has anyone accused you of wrong when you knew beyond any doubt that you were innocent? What was your reaction?

WORD WEALTH

hope (Job 4:6), *tiqvah* (teek-*vah*); Strong's #8615: Hope; expectation; something yearned for and anticipated eagerly; something for which one waits. *Tiqvah* comes from the verb *qavah,* meaning "to wait for" or "to look hopefully" in a particular direction. Its original meaning was "to stretch like a rope." In Joshua 2:18, 21, it is translated "line" or "cord"; Rahab was instructed to tie a scarlet *tiqvah* (cord or rope) in her window as her hope for rescue. Yahweh Himself is the hope of the godly (Ps. 71:5). Here Eliphaz acknowledges that integrity should be the basis of a person's hope.[5]

WORD WEALTH

mortal (Job 4:17) is translated from the word *'enosh,* denoting man in his frailty, limitation, and imperfection. It stands in contrast to *geber* which was used in Job 3:3 to refer to a man at the height of his strength. *'Enosh* is derived from a word meaning "to be frail, sick, weak, and sad." In Dan. 7:13, the Aramaic equivalent *bar'enash* (Son of Man) is a messianic term. By repeatedly calling himself "Son of Man," the Lord Jesus identified with the human race in its weaknesses, yet rises to a position of everlasting strength.[6]

WORD WEALTH

trouble (Job 5:7), *'amal* (ah-*mahl*); Strong's #5999; Sorrow, labor, toil, grief, pain, trouble, misery, fatigue, exhaustion. This noun occurs fifty-six times in the Old Testament. Its root is the verb *'amal,* "to labor or toil to the point of exhaustion."[7] It refers to the drudgery of toil and the unfulfilling aspects of work and is often used in parallelism with *yagon,* "torment, sorrow" (Jer. 20:18); *ka`as,* "provocation" (Ps. 10:14); *'oni,* "misery" (Deut. 26:7); *'awen,* "trouble" (Ps. 90:10); and *shaw',* "worthlessness" (Job 7:3).[8]

FAITH ALIVE

Growing in Godliness (Job 5:17). Godliness will result from a true knowledge of God. Godly living rejects evil attitudes and looks for God in every circumstance.

Avoid resentment, lack of forgiveness, and envy. Believe that these are self-destructive attitudes. Embrace the Lord's correction. Consider it a blessing. Know that it evidences the Lord's love for you.[9]

In Job's response to Eliphaz (Job 6—7) he declares that his protest is just and continues his lament, expressing terror at his unexplained suffering. Job also considers how his friends (6:8–30) and God (7:7–21) are related to his present circumstances.

Read through Job 6. Count the number of times the word "taste" occurs. What is being "tasted" in each instance?

In what ways does Job directly address his friend's argument? (6:8–30)

Contrast Job's invitation to his friends to *look at him* (6:28) with Eliphaz' conclusion from general observation (4:7, 8; 5:27). Describe how your perspective about an issue has changed when faced with a "real live person" instead of general statistics.

In Job 7:11–21, Job addresses God directly. Of what does Job accuse God?

Job 7:17 recalls to mind Psalm 8:4. Yet Job presents a very different experience of life lived under the watchful eye of God. How does Job's understanding enlarge or change the vision of Psalm 8:4–8?

Under what circumstances do you wish God would not pay so much attention to you (see Job 7:17–19)? Why?

PRESERVED BY GOD

Bildad (Job 8) is shocked at Job's seeming insolence: How can Job accuse God of being unjust? List the ways in which Bildad upholds God's innocence.

The rhetorical questions in verse 3 are meant by Bildad to direct Job to the "tried and true" answers. In Job's context, how might they sound to Job? How are these questions helpful to Job?

Do you think Bildad is insensitive to Job's grief over the death of his sons? (8:4)

According to Bildad, what should Job do? (8:5)

Reflect on Bildad's appeal to tradition as a source of authority in 8:8–10. How should believers view the traditions of past generations? What is the relationship between tradition and present experience?

Compare the last sentence of Bildad's speech (8:22) with the last sentence of Job's previous speech (7:21). What is the basis of Bildad's hope for Job? Is it a legitimate basis?

Job's response to Bildad (chs. 9—10) reveals the deep agony of Job's suffering. Job honestly feels he is innocent. Yet he tenaciously holds onto God and pleads with Him.

Job's response addresses some issues raised in Eliphaz' first speech (chs. 4—5). How does Job reinterpret the creative activity of God? (see 5:9–16 and 9:4–13)

Reflect on Job's description of God in 9:4–13. What does this reveal about Job's faith in God?

In the light of God's overwhelming strength and superior wisdom (9:4–13), Job longs for a common ground like a court setting in which to speak to God (9:32–35). Chapter 10 records Job's hypothetical remarks to God if such a setting existed. Job returns here to the themes of creation and birth (compare 3:1–26).

List the questions which Job asks of God in chapter 10. How does Job seek for a common ground with God through these questions?

List the ways in which Job recognizes the blessings of God in his life. (10:8–12)

How do these recognized blessings add to the confusion of Job? How does Job use them in his speech to God?

It is important that we recognize the blessings of God in our lives during difficult times. List the ways in which God has blessed your life recently.

WORD WEALTH

preserved (Job 10:12), *shamar* (shah-*mar*); Strong's #8104; To guard, keep, protect, preserve; watch over, care for, safekeep. The earliest use of *shamar* is Genesis 2:15, where Adam was to tend and keep the Garden of Eden. People are instructed to guard the covenant, the Sabbath, and the commandments (Gen. 17:9; Ex. 31:14; Deut. 28:9). The participle *shomer* means "he who watches," that is, a watchman or shepherd. The Lord is called *shomer Yisrael,* the "One who guards Israel." This Watchman never slumbers and never sleeps but is always on duty (Ps. 121:4).[10]

DIVINE GREATNESS AND HUMAN FRAILTY

Zophar speaks for the first time and challenges Job's pride (Job 11). His speech is not so much against Job's logic as it is against Job's character.

Review Zophar's speech in chapter 11. Trace how Zophar uses the theme of hiddenness. Compare its use here with Eliphaz' words in 5:9 and Job's response in 9:5–10.

According to Zophar, what should Job do? (Job 11:13–15)

How does the giving of advice contradict what Zophar has just said about the "deep things" of God?

How does Zophar's counsel (11:13–19) compare to Bildad's (9:4–7)?

Note how Zophar picks up Job's earlier words and turns them around (11:13–20):

Compare verse 15a with 9:27 (face)

Compare verse 15b with 3:25 (fear)

Compare verse 16a with 3:10, 20 (misery)

Compare verse 16b with 6:15 (waters)

Compare verse 17 with 10:21, 22 (darkness/light)

Compare verses 18–20 with 3:26; 6:11–13; 7:4–6 (rest/hope)

In the light of the revelation of God, which is held until chapters 38—41, to what extent is Zophar correct:

about God's hiddenness?

about Job's sinfulness?

Job responds for the third time (12:1—14:22) and begins with a long speech about God's attributes. Job's point is not that he knows as much about God as his friends know. Sure, Job is not ignorant of their arguments. But it is precisely their arguments about God's greatness which complicate his own problem. Thus, Job turns the words of his friends around in a mocking description of traditional wisdom (12:2–12) and the hidden wisdom of God (12:13–25).

How does Job answer the words of Zophar (11:7–9) in 12:7–10?

List the ways in which God is accused by Job of misusing His wisdom and creative power (12:13–25).

WORD WEALTH

strength (Job 12:16), *'oz (aoz);* Strong's #5797; strength, power, security. This word occurs primarily in reference to God. Strength is an inherent characteristic of God and is shown in His voice (Ps. 68:33) and His arm (Is. 62:8). The strength of the Lord provides security and protection for the righteous.[11] In this reference, God's strength is contrasted with human weakness (see Job 14).

In Job 13:7, Job asks his friends if they are speaking wickedly for God. He believes their religion is a "cover up" for God. To what extent do you think this is true?

What "truth" is Job concerned to protect?

Job 13:15 records Job's well-known words of trust, "Though He slay me, yet will I trust Him." What irony is involved in this statement?

What is the basis of Job's hope in this statement?

How does Job's willingness to be slain by God answer Satan's question of Job in Job 1:9?

Job's third response shifts from God's strength to humanity's frailty (13:28—14:22). In 14:1–12, Job reflects on the shortness of life. How does the experience of pain and suffering raise this question in your own life?

How is the brevity of life masked in our culture?

Respond to Job's assessment of the finality of death. (Job 14:13–22)

For what does Job hope in Job 14:15?

FAITH ALIVE

When everything else seems to fail, confidence in God's character is the bottom line. Job was so convinced of the redemptive nature of God (see 19:25), that he would trust in God even in the face of death. The issue of faith rests in God's ability to perform, while the action of faith rests in one's ability to believe. The ability to believe is given to every person (Rom. 12:3); how one uses this ability will determine the kind of relationship one will have with the God for whom nothing is impossible.[12]

What situations cause your faith to be tested?

Ask God to increase your faith.

1. C.S. Lewis, *A Grief Observed* (New York: Bantam Books, 1961), 1.

2. *Spirit-Filled Life® Bible* (Nashville: Thomas Nelson Publishers, 1991), 1104, "Word Wealth: Jeremiah 31:22, man."

3. Ibid., 749, "Truth-In-Action through Job."

4. Ibid., 713, note on Job 4:1—5:27.

5. Ibid., 1260, "Word Wealth: Hosea 2:15, hope."

6. Ibid., 714, "Word Wealth: Job 4:17, mortal."

7. Ibid., "Word Wealth: Job 5:7, trouble."

8. *Theological Wordbook of the Old Testament,* Vol 1 (Chicago: Moody Press, 1980), 675.

9. *Spirit-Filled Life® Bible,* 748, "Truth-in-Action through Job."

10. Ibid., 719, "Word Wealth: Job 10:12, preserved."

11. *Theological Wordbook of the Old Testament,* Vol. 1, 659–660.

12. *Hayford's Bible Handbook* (Nashville: Thomas Nelson Publishers, 1995), 133, note on Job 13:15.

Lesson 3/Job's Hope
Job 15—21

"For we were saved in this hope, but hope that is seen is not hope; for why does one still hope for what he sees?"

—Romans 8:24

"Hope is the passion for the impossible."

—Jacques Ellul[1]

Most of us use the word "hope" lightly. "I hope you have a good day," we might tell a friend. A mother encourages her daughter, "I hope you do well on your exam." A father hopes his son will do well in sports. Parents hope that life will be better for their children. All these desires are fine and good, but they all exist within the realm of *possibilities*. They are more like goals to work for and attain than realities which lie completely outside of human attainment, which is what hope is all about.

Job's story is a perfect illustration of hope. When all of life came crashing down around him, and all human possibilities were exhausted, hope sprang up in Job's soul. Like Abraham, "who, contrary to hope, in hope believed," (Rom. 4:18), Job trusted in an unseen Redeemer (Job 19:25, 26).

THE FOLLY OF THE WICKED

Eliphaz has listened to Job and is now on the defensive. Job has challenged his traditional beliefs and his concept of God, and now, in his second speech (Job 15), Eliphaz becomes severe in his reprimands of Job.

What does Eliphaz think of Job's previous words? (vv. 2–4)

What does Eliphaz think of Job? (vv. 5, 6; contrast Job 9:20a)

 PROBING THE DEPTHS

The rhetorical questions of Eliphaz in verses 7 and 8 echo the passage about wisdom in Proverbs 8:22–31 (see especially vv. 25, 31). Eliphaz intends the questions to be stinging accusations of Job's arrogance. Job's situation, however, if compared to the pre-creation darkness of Genesis 1:2, allows for the possibility of turning these questions into pointers toward a deeper truth. Those who suffer innocently are made privy to the wisdom which existed "before the hills" were made. And they are in a place where creative things can happen again.

Read Proverbs 8:31. Recall times in your life when the creative wisdom of God "rejoiced" in you. Were those the times you "had it all together" or were you, like Job, in the middle of seemingly impossible difficulties?

Eliphaz feels the need to repeat what he has said earlier in Job 4:17–19. What is the theology of Eliphaz concerning humanity and righteousness? (see 15:14–16) Do you agree or disagree with these statements?

 FAITH ALIVE

Developing Humility (Job 15:14). The true knowledge of God leads to humility. Humility is not the self-deprecation with which many of us are often acquainted. Rather, it is the refusal to trust oneself for fulfillment of needs, looking instead to the Lord.

Understand that one's own righteousness is a vain hope. Believe that only Christ's imputed righteousness can allow us to stand before God. Diligently avoid any form of self-righteousness. Understand that it makes one unteachable and unshapable in God's hand. Humble yourself regularly in the presence of the Lord. Do not be hasty to reply against God.[2]

How does the conclusion of Eliphaz' second speech (15:17–35) differ from that of his first (5:17–27) with regard to his advice for Job?

In Job 15:25, Eliphaz implies that Job has "stretched out his hand against God." In the light of Job 1:11, 12 and 2:3–6, who has actually stretched out his hand against whom?

EMPTY COMFORT

The response of Job to Eliphaz is addressed to all three of his friends (16:1–5). Why does Job call them miserable comforters? (v. 2)

If the tables were turned, would Job really give comfort to his friends with his words? (16:4, 5)

In Job 6:6, Job expresses the frustration of not knowing whether to speak out or to keep silent in his pain. Yet he keeps speaking. Do you withdraw from speaking when you are in pain? Is this helpful? Why or why not?

Whom does Job perceive to be his "adversary"? (6:9)

How has Job's condition affected him socially? (16:7–22; 17:6–9)

FAITH ALIVE

Compare Job's reputation before his calamities (Job 1:3) with his social position at this point in the story. Job longs for his friends to understand and to confirm or "witness" how he understands things. All of us need to be known the way we perceive ourselves to be. Recall times when people avoided you or misunderstood you. Compare your feelings with Job's. Were their actions a commentary on any wrongdoing on your part or on their lack of true concern?

WORD WEALTH

Wound (Job 16:14) translates *peres,* a forceful word denoting a destructive breach or rupture. The verb form is used of the destruction of the walls of Jerusalem by the Babylonians. When God is the subject, the word describes His punitive activity upon a group or individual.[3] In this passage, repetition increases the force of the meaning. A literal reading is, "He bursts upon me with burst upon burst."

BIBLE EXTRA

In Job 17:3, Job asks God to "make a pledge" with him. The language is similar in Proverbs 11:15; 17:18; and 22:26, all of which warn against entering financial agreements rashly. Job's point is that since his friends will not support him, he asks God to be his surety.

Read Job 17:6–16. What signs are revealed in this passage that Job has a new sense of energy and hope?

verse 9

verse 10

verses 13–16

THE PUNISHMENT OF THE WICKED

Bildad's second speech (Job 18) is a tirade against evildoers, but in reality he means Job. Bildad no longer mentions the possibility of Job's repentance. Death and destruction await the wicked. It is intended as a harsh warning to Job and strikes Job at a deep emotional level.

How does Bildad address Job's concern about death? (Review Job 17:13–16.)

 BIBLE EXTRA

Bildad accuses Job of regarding his friends as animals (18:3). This human–animal comparison is a theme which runs throughout the book. Look up Job 5:22, 23; 6:5; 11:12; 12:7–9; 38:39—39:40; 40:15—41:34. What do you believe is the significance of this comparison?

Compare the punishments of the wicked named by Bildad in this speech with those of Achan in Joshua 7:15.

Read Job 18. List the ways in which Bildad makes the point that the wicked will have no place upon the earth?

How does Bildad's assessment respond to Job's request in 16:18 for the earth to preserve his blood and provide a place for his cry? (See 18:16–21.)

 ### Word Wealth

world (Job 18:18), *tebel* (teh-*vel*); Strong's #8398: The fruitful earth; the globe, the world, the dry land; earth's substantial material (land); also the entire world (that is, all its inhabitants). *Tebel* occurs thirty-six times. God formed or established the world. The primary idea is land in general, or inhabited world (Prov. 8:31). The root of *tebel* is *yabal,* "to bring," which may imply earth that produces.[4]

A Redeemer Kinsman

Job answers Bildad's "How long?" (18:2) with his own "How long?" (19:1). Job's question to his friends here is: "How long will you keep tormenting me when God is already doing a fine job of it?"

Review chapter 19, noting the theme of estrangement. List the various persons Job considers cut off from him.

Word Wealth

The Hebrew word translated "soul" in Job 19:2 is the same as the word translated "life" in Job 2:5, 6, where Satan is instructed to "spare his life." In essence, Job's friends were not sparing his life or soul with their words, but were hurting him more deeply than his physical condition. Words can hurt!

At the end of his lament, when Job perceives himself to be isolated and physically emaciated, Job's profound hope shines through (19:25–27). His Redeemer lives! Such tenacious faith gives even deeper meaning to his passionate lament.

AT A GLANCE

Note the reversal of two themes in Job 19
vv. 5–22	vv. 23–29
isolation from relatives	————hope in a kinsman-redeemer
flesh is wasted	————————will see God in his flesh

Job has already hinted at a belief in resurrection in Job 14:13–15. How does this passage (19:23–29) advance Job's vision?

BEHIND THE SCENES

In ancient Israel, the kinsman-redeemer was the nearest of kin who acted to buy back the freedom of a family member who had fallen into slavery, or to avenge the blood of a relative who had been murdered. Job's statement is even more significant because he feels abandoned by all earthly kinsmen.

BIBLE EXTRA

Job 19:25, 26 is one of the Old Testament's greatest prophetic affirmations of an anticipated Redeemer/Savior who will bring hope of a literal, physical resurrection to redeemed humankind.[5]

Look up 1 Corinthians 15:35–49. How does the New Testament understanding of resurrection compare with Job's statements here?

It is Job's hope to "see God" (vv. 26, 27). Notice the repetition of "see," and "behold." What significance does this particular hope have in the light of Job's previous perceptions of his relationship with God?

> **flesh** (Job 19:26), *basar* (bah-*sar*); Strong's #1320:
> Flesh, body, human being. *Kol basar,* "all flesh," means all
> humanity together (see Joel 2:28). *Basar* refers to the human
> body and is never used to refer to God. The first occurrence
> of *basar* is in Genesis 2:21, where God closed up the sleep-
> ing man's "flesh" after extracting one rib. The simplest mean-
> ing is "the visible part of humans or animals," that is, the skin,
> muscle, flesh, and so on.[6]

Job concludes this speech with a warning to his friends to
beware of the judgment of God. If God is on Job's side, they
will be punished. In what way is Job expressing hope for himself in these statements?

THE PROSPERITY OF THE WICKED

Zophar, in his second speech (Job 20), continues the
same argument of Job's other friends: although the wicked
may seem to prosper, eventually they will suffer in the end.
Thus Job must have some hidden sin for which he is now
being punished.

Job's words have shaken up the tightly controlled, cause-
and-effect world of Zophar. List the ways in which Zophar
reveals that he is threatened by Job. (vv. 2, 3)

PROBING THE DEPTHS

> Zophar (Job 20:1–29) speaks about the devastating end
> of the wicked person and the hypocrite, including Job in those
> categories (vv. 4–29). Zophar is narrow-minded and legalistic,
> with no mercy for Job. He does not know how to answer Job's
> questions and is indignant at Job's accusations toward his
> friends.[7]

In what way does Zophar appeal to history and tradition
in his argument? (Job 20:4)

In Job 20:8–11, how does Zophar attempt to reverse Job's vision of resurrection?

AT A GLANCE

Bildad (Job 18) and Zophar (Job 20) are similar in how they present the outcome of the wicked. Note the following parallels.

Chapter 18	Chapter 20
earth will not be shaken for the wicked (v. 4)	earth will stand up against the wicked (v. 27)
wicked expelled from his tent (v. 14)	food expelled from the wicked (v. 15)
death gnaws on bones of the wicked (v. 13)	viper's tongue will slay the wicked (v. 16)
wicked driven from light into darkness (v. 18)	darkness is reserved for treasures of wicked (v. 26)
tent of wicked destroyed (v. 15)	belongings of tent carried away (vv. 26, 28)
no trace will be left of the wicked (vv. 15–19)	the wicked will be cut down by God's wrath (vv. 23–25)
this is the dwelling/ place of the wicked (v. 21)	this is the portion/heritage of the wicked (v. 29)[8]

After reading Bildad's and Zophar's account of the wicked, it becomes clear that they are teaching that "the punishment fits the crime." To what extent is this true of all sinfulness?

Why is a theology of retribution (as illustrated by Bildad and Zophar) true on one level, yet not true on another?

Remember Satan's challenge to God in Job 1:9–11? Review this passage. Notice how the removal of God's hedge of protection (house and possessions) corresponds with the punishments of house and possessions enumerated by Bildad and Zophar.

    AT A GLANCE

A comparison of Satan's theology with that of Job's friends[9]

Satan	Friends
IF Job is blessed by God, THEN he will be faithful	IF Job is faithful, THEN he will be blessed
OR	OR
IF Job is not blessed by God, THEN he will not be faithful (Satan accused God of bribing Job)	IF Job is unfaithful, THEN he will be punished

PROBING THE DEPTHS

In chapter 21, Job appeals for a hearing (vv. 1–6) to challenge the oversimplified doctrine of retribution (vv. 7–33). He again confirms his own innocence; calamity falls on the just and unjust, a truth that history confirms. Sometimes the ungodly prosper throughout life while the godly know little except want. Here the subject moves from a focus on Job specifically to the larger question of the suffering of the godly. Thus Job challenges the major theological view of the day.[10]

In Job 21:22–26, Job argues that both the strong (materially prosperous) and the weak (materially poor) die just alike. How does this refute the argument of Zophar in Job 20:5–29?

In Job 21:27–33, Job argues that the tents of the wicked are not destroyed but merely replaced with tombs in which they are remembered. How does this refute Bildad's argument in Job 18:5–21?

Job has the courage to challenge the accepted theological view concerning suffering and prosperity. What other figures in the Bible or throughout church history have refuted the so-called "correct" beliefs of their day to reveal the deeper truths of God?

Doctrines are important to the total life of the church. They are not, however, to be given more authority than Scripture as it is interpreted in the community of believers who are submitted to the Holy Spirit. What teachings have you struggled with as you matured in your walk with the Lord?

How can the church become more sensitive to the questions of its members in a way which invites critical reflection on its own teachings without giving in to the philosophy of "anything goes"?

 BIBLE EXTRA

James 5:11 speaks of the "patience of Job," yet in Job 21:4, Job speaks of his "impatience" (literally, "shortness of breath/spirit"). The entire story of Job reveals that Job is, indeed, patient. His is a patience which goes on and does not give up even in the face of his own "impatience." Job reminds

us of other biblical characters. Look up the following passages. How are these people like or unlike Job?

Jeremiah 12:1–4 (Jeremiah)

Habakkuk 3:17, 19 (Habakkuk)

Luke 11:5–9 (Importunate friend)

Luke 18:1–8 (Importunate widow)

James 5:4 (Oppressed laborers)

James 5:8 (You!)

1. Jacques Ellul, *Hope in Time of Abandonment* (New York: The Seabury Press, 1977), 197.
2. *Spirit-Filled Life® Bible* (Nashville: Thomas Nelson Publishers, 1991), 748, "Truth-in-Action through Job."
3. *Theological Wordbook of the Old Testament*, Vol. II (Chicago: Moody Press, 1980), 737.
4. *Spirit-Filled Life® Bible*, 1134, "Word Wealth: Jeremiah 51:15, world."
5. Ibid., 726, note on Job 19:25, 26.
6. Ibid., 727, "Word Wealth: Job 19:26, flesh."
7. Ibid., note on Job 20:1–29.
8. J. Gerald Janzen, *Job* (Interpretation Commentary, Atlanta: John Knox Press, 1985), 153.
9. *Nelson's Complete Book of Bible Maps and Charts: Old and New Testaments* (Nashville: Thomas Nelson Publishers, 1993), 173.
10. Ibid., 728, note on Job 21:1–34.

Lesson 4/Job's Perseverance
Job 22—26

In the famous Battle of the Bulge in World War II, General Anthony C. McAuliffe had been ordered to hold the Belgian road hub of Bastogne against the hostile Nazi counteroffensive. Although outnumbered four to one, with food and supplies almost exhausted, he and his 10,000 men endured the bitter winter winds of 1944 and withstood the heavily armed German troops.

After several days, the Germans sent an officer to deliver an ultimatum to surrender. McAuliffe responded with the message, "To the German Commander—Nuts!" After five more grueling days of fighting, the siege was finally broken. General George S. Patton, the rescuing commander, awarded General McAuliffe the Distinguished Service Cross in honor of McAuliffe's dedicated perseverance.[1]

Job persisted through his ordeal, even when his friends accused him of wrongdoing. Sometimes the fight of faith requires perseverance which seems outside our abilities. It is then that God enables us to endure.

COMING FORTH AS GOLD

The third and last speech by Eliphaz (Job 22) repeats once again the argument of the three friends: Job must be a horrible sinner to be suffering so much. In this final speech, however, he aims specific accusations directly at Job.

In the light of God's words about Job in Job 1:8–12; 2:3–6, what is the answer to Eliphaz' questions in 22:2, 3?

What will God gain if Job remains faithful?

In verse 4 the word "corrects" could also be translated "proves." In the light of Job 1:1, 8, what is the answer to Eliphaz' question about Job's fear of the Lord?

List the sins with which Eliphaz accuses Job. (vv. 5–20)

If Eliphaz has no basis for these accusations except for his perception of God's wrath toward Job, why do you think he accuses Job of such things? Is Eliphaz "backed in a corner" and "grasping for straws"?

Contrast the "peace" which Eliphaz promises Job (22:21) with the "peace" which Job actually seeks. Which "peace" is most congruent with reality?

 WORD WEALTH

Almighty (Job 22:23), *shadday* (shad-*dye*); Strong's #7706: All-powerful; when it appears as *'El Shadday,* it is "God Almighty." This name occurs about fifty times in the Old Testament. The patriarchs knew God by this name (Gen. 17:1; Ex. 6:3). Some trace its origin to the verb *shadad,* meaning "mighty, unconquerable." Others relate the word to the Akkadian word for "mountain," indicating God's greatness, strength, or His everlasting nature. Another possible explanation is that *Shadday* is a compound of the particle *shey* (which or who) and *day* (sufficient). *Shey-day* or *Shadday* is therefore the all-sufficient God, eternally capable of being all that His people need.[2]

In Job 22:24, 25, Eliphaz uses the imagery of gold. He argues that if Job will lay his "gold" in the dust (i.e., his pride or claims of innocence), God will become his gold. In Job's response to Eliphaz (Job 23:10), Job uses the same imagery of gold. He repudiates Eliphaz' advice, however, holding to his claim that he will not lay down his claim to his integrity because that would be a lie. He will come forth as "gold."

Eliphaz claims that if Job repents, God will deliver him and will perhaps use him to pray for others who are not innocent (see Job 22:30). What irony do you see in this statement in the light of what actually happened later as recorded in Job 42:7–10?

Job's "complaint" in chapter 23 includes a cry to "find" God (vv. 3–9). Under what circumstances do you most identify with Job in this cry?

Although Job cannot find God, does Job believe God knows where he, Job, is? (see v. 10) Which is more important, knowing where God is or knowing that God knows where we are?

Instead of "finding" God, what has Job found? (v. 17)

UNPUNISHED EVIL

In chapter 24, Job turns his attention away from his own problems and asks questions on behalf of all those who seem to suffer without cause. Before you read this passage, list current instances of unjust suffering of which you are aware, whether in your neighborhood or around the world.

Describe your emotional reaction to verses 2–12.

Which of the particular injustices which Job names do you see in the world today?

What questions would you ask God about these situations?

   WORD WEALTH

---

needy (Job 24:4), *'ebyon* (ehv-*yoan*); Strong's #34: One in need; a destitute, lacking, or poor individual. The Law of God required that the poor should receive just treatment (Ex. 23:6). The prophets strongly denounced those who abuse or oppress needy persons (Amos 4:1; Ezek. 22:29–31). God is the special Protector of the needy (Is. 25:4). Jesus proclaimed, "The poor have the gospel preached to them" (Matt. 11:5).[3] Concern for the needy is one of the hallmarks of God's people.

Do you agree or disagree with Job's conclusion in verse 12 that "God does not charge them with wrong" (meaning "God sees nothing amiss")? Why or why not?

Verses 13–17 speaks of the audacity of the wicked to commit evil in the light of day. Summarize their attitude toward light and toward darkness. Contrast these verses with Job's earlier words in 23:15–17.

Job presents the view of his friends in verses 18–21 (review chs. 18, 20), then he refutes that view in verses 22–24. Compare Job's statements in Job 21:32, 33. It seems that the wicked go to their graves like everyone else without receiving punishment. Do you agree or disagree? Why or why not?

  PROBING THE DEPTHS

In a lengthy soliloquy (Job 24:1–25), Job complains against the violence God permits to occur in the earth, such as the oppression of the innocent and the persecution of the defenseless by evildoers. He calls attention to the murderer and adulterer who perform their deeds in secret and seem to escape speedy judgment; in fact, it appears that God grants them security. It appears his own suffering has made him more sensitive to evil and general human suffering. Essentially, Job debates the age-old questions: How can a righteous God allow the ungodly to prosper? And, why is there such a long delay in their punishment?[4]

Reflect on your understanding of God's punishment of the wicked in the world today. In what ways may it be said that evil persons do receive punishment from God in this life?

BEHOLDING GOD'S MAJESTY

Bildad's final speech (Job 25) is cut short by Job who will hear no more arguments. Then in language which is highly poetic and moving, Job offers his own rendition of God's majesty in the created order (Job 26:5–13).

Psalm 8 has already been used by Job in Job 7:17–21. Here, in chapter 25, Bildad offers his own interpretation of Psalm 8. Read Psalm 8 and compare with Bildad's comments. How has Bildad changed the meaning of Psalm 8?

What similarities do you see in chapter 25 with the previous speeches of Eliphaz?

Job 4:17–19

Job 15:14–16

How does Bildad characterize humanity in verses 4–6?

In his response to Bildad, how does Job characterize humanity? (Job 26:2, 3)

According to the following topics, describe Job's rendition of God's majesty in creation. (Job 26)

earth (vv. 5–7)

water, sea (vv. 5, 8, 10, 12)

heaven (vv. 11, 13)

Compare Job's picture of creation with Genesis 1—2 and with Psalm 104. What similarities and differences do you see?

BIBLE EXTRA

Destruction (Job 26:6) can be translated "Abaddon," a metaphoric name for the grave.[5] Compare the use of the word in the following verses:

Job 28:22

Job 31:12

Psalm 88:11

Proverbs 15:11

PROBING THE DEPTHS

Although what Job says here (26:5–14) is true, the context implies that Job intends this speech to be a parody of his friend's speeches about God. In essence, Job claims to be able to do a better job of describing God's omnipotence. Look ahead to God's speeches in Job 38—41. There God reveals his omnipotence to Job "in person." In chapter 26, Job speaks dramatically about God's power, but his words about God are not enough to satisfy Job's questioning heart.

What are the implications for those who know about God's power but have never experienced God *"in person"*?

If Job describes the wonders of creation as "the mere edges" of God's ways, what do you think he meant by "the thunder of His power"? (v. 14)

In the light of verse 14, describe the difference between admiring God's majestic handiwork in creation and experiencing God's presence in worship.

1. Richard Anderson, "For Example" (St. Louis: Concordia Publishing House, 1977), 159, 160.
2. *Spirit-Filled Life® Bible* (Nashville: Thomas Nelson Publishers, 1991), 833, "Word Wealth: Psalm 91, Almighty."
3. Ibid., 812, "Word Wealth: Psalm 70:5, needy."
4. Ibid., 730, 732, note on Job 24:1–25.
5. Ibid., 732, note on Job 26:6.

Lesson 5/Job's Integrity
Job 27—31

In March 1861, Abraham Lincoln was inaugurated as the sixteenth president of the United States during one of the most critical times in its history. Seven states had already seceded from the union, and with the first gunshots at Fort Sumter, South Carolina, on April 12, 1861, the Civil War began.

Throughout the first years of the war, Lincoln led the Union through battle after battle with grim determination. He became noted for his vigorous measures, often going against the advice of his military commanders and stretching the Constitution to its limits.

Lincoln lived with a deep sense of personal integrity during this national crisis as his following statements reveal: "I desire so to conduct the affairs of this administration that if at the end, when I come to lay down the reins of power, I have lost every other friend on earth, I shall at least have one friend left, and that friend shall be down inside of me." Again, he said, "I do the very best I know how; the very best I can; and I mean to keep on doing it to the end. If the end brings me out all right, what is said against me will not amount to anything. If the end brings me out all wrong, then a legion of angels swearing I was right will make no difference."[1]

Although Lincoln gave the command of the army to Ulysses S. Grant in 1864, he still maintained a vision of national unity until his untimely death. He died with a copy of General William Sherman's orders for the March to the Sea in his pocket. His integrity had served him well.

WISDOM'S WAYS

Job 27 may be divided into two sections. Verses 1–12 are attributed to Job, and verses 13–23 are sometimes attributed to one of Job's three friends, usually Zophar, whose last speech ended (Job 20:29) with almost the identical words of 27:13. It is also possible to view verses 1–12 as a quotation from Job of what he anticipates Zophar might say next. If the latter is the case, then Zophar does not actually have a third speech.

The ambiguity in the text at this point indicates that the dialogues of Job and his three friends have broken down. Job has already cut Bildad's last speech short. Now Zophar does not get a proper introduction and perhaps not even a chance to speak for himself.

In 27:1–12, Job continues to maintain his innocence. Reflect on the tensions of this section.

List Job's accusations of God.

List Job's statements of belief and trust in God.

In verses 1–6, Job speaks an oath which is like a curse called upon himself if what he states is not true. Oaths are found throughout many parts of Scripture. According to the following topics, describe the similarities of Job's oath and the oath of Paul in Romans 9:1.

Spirit/Breath of God

False speaking

God/Christ

What is Job defending in his oath? (Job 27:1–6)

verse 2

verse 5

verse 6

How does this oath answer the question asked by Job's wife in Job 1:9?

How does this oath answer the challenge of Satan to God in Job 2:2–6?

To what extent do you believe Job's oath to be a statement of faith in God?

In your own words, define Job's "integrity." (v. 5)

The fragment of Zophar's (anticipated?) speech (27:13–23) repeats what the three friends have consistently maintained. The wicked will come to ruin. Describe the difference between "Zophar's" account of the death of the wicked (vv. 19–23) and Job's assessment in Job 21:32, 33 and 24:22–24.

The dialogues having ended, Job now speaks in soliloquy on the value and source of wisdom (ch. 28). The chapter may be divided into three sections: wisdom cannot be found in earthly places (vv. 1–14); wisdom cannot be bought (vv. 15–22); wisdom is found only in God (vv. 23–28).

Read verses 1–11 and list the precious materials named here which humans have discovered in the earth.

According to verse 3, what do humans explore in order to find these precious materials?

In the light of Job's use of darkness as a theme in his speeches (for examples, see 3:6; 10:22; 23:17), how might Job himself be thought of as a miner?

How might God be thought of as a miner? (Remember Job 12:22 and 23:10! See also 28:23.)

How is Job's experience reflected in verse 4?

How might Job's experiences be described as his "being turned up [transformed] as by fire"? (v. 5)

Although humans can find wealth in the earth, can they, according to Job, find wisdom in the earthly realm? (vv. 12–14)

Read verses 15–19 and list all the verbs related to buying and selling.

According to Job, can humans purchase wisdom? (vv. 15–19)

BEHIND THE SCENES

The gold of Ophir is mentioned in Job 28:16. The location of Ophir is unknown. Suggestions of its location span from Africa to India.

 ## FAITH ALIVE

According to society today, there is great wisdom in technology and in commerce. Much value is placed on developing better and more efficient ways of producing goods ("mining") and in shrewd business practices to earn profits ("gold, silver and precious stones"). Job solidly refutes such ideas.

Why does our society place such high value on technology and business?

How should the believer view technology and consumerism?

In your opinion, what role should the church play in teaching the value of godly wisdom in the midst of a consumer-driven society?

Job completes his speech about wisdom by focusing on the creative activity of God. (Job 28:23–28) List the four activities of God named here which are beyond human comprehension.

wind (v. 25)

waters (v. 25)

rain (v. 26)

lightning (v. 26)

List the four actions God performed in relation to wisdom. (v. 27)

According to verses 24–27, when does wisdom come into being?

Can humans bring such wisdom into being?

How can humans participate in the wisdom of God? (v. 28)

 PROBING THE DEPTHS

In his discourse on wisdom (Job 28:1–28), Job affirms that only true wisdom brings well-being. This wisdom lies in God who alone can resolve the unanswered questions of life. Humanity's solution is to find peace through submission to divine authority.[2]

 WORD WEALTH

Wisdom (Job 28:12) is used in the Old Testament to cover the entire range of human experience, from the skill required for making garments for the high priest (Ex. 28:3) to the wisdom of governmental leaders (Deut. 34:9). The verb, "be wise," represents a manner of thinking and attitude or disposition toward life's experiences. In the ancient Near East, wisdom was understood as a practical pursuit.[3] In this passage, Job reflects the wisdom tradition of the Israelites. God is the source of wisdom, and wisdom begins with "the fear of the Lord" (Job 28:28).

BIBLE EXTRA

Compare Job's discussion of seeking for wisdom (Job 28:12) with the promise of wisdom in the story of the Garden of Eden in Genesis 2—3.

How might Job's experiences be compared to the tree of temptation in Genesis 2—3?

How might the voice of Job's friends calling him to repent be compared to the voice of the serpent in Genesis 3?

How does Job's reaction to his friends differ from the couple's reaction to the serpent in Genesis 3?

Describe the different outcomes of the two stories.[4]

MEMORY WITHOUT HOPE

The twin themes of memory and hope have consistently been a part of Israelite faith. Remembering what God has done in the past and looking forward to what God will do in the future are important for living faithfully in the present. In chapters 29 and 30, Job remembers, but he does not anticipate a future. According to the following topics, describe Job's happy memories recorded in the following sections:

His life with God (29:1–6)

His reputation (29:7–11)

His community service (29:12–17)

His former hopes (29:18–20)

His community leadership (29:21–25)

 PROBING THE DEPTHS

Job reviews his former prosperity (29:1–10); he states that this prosperity was a direct result of his lifestyle of piety and benevolence (29:11–17); he speaks of his former expectation that this prosperity would continue until his death (29:18–25). Job directs attention to the disdain he now suffers from men in contrast to the high honor he received formerly (30:1–15). He recognizes his present miserable state and considers all his hopes for the future to be lost.[5]

 WORD WEALTH

blessed (Job 29:11), 'ashar (ah-shar); Strong's #833: Happy, blessed, prosperous, successful, straight, right, contented. Originally, the word meant "be straight." When Leah gave birth to a son, she said, "I am happy, for the daughters will call me blessed" (Gen. 30:13). She named this son "Asher" (from 'ashar), meaning "Happy One." Both the Messiah and the nation of Israel will be called "blessed" ('ashar) by the world: "Men shall be blessed in Him; all nations shall call Him blessed" (Ps. 72:17). "And all nations will call you blessed, for you will be a delightful land" (Mal. 3:12).[6]

In contrast to his blessed past, Job describes his present state of misery in chapter 30. In several ways, his present has become a reversal of his past. According to the following topics, describe Job's present condition.

identification with the unwanted (30:1–8)

rejection by the unwanted (30:9–15)

physical condition (30:16–19)

perception of God (30:20–23)

emotional/psychological state (30:24–31)

 WORD WEALTH

In Job 30:19, the verb for "cast" can also mean "teach," or "instruct." In a similar way, the verb "have become" can carry the idea of comparison or likening to. In other words, God's action of casting Job into the mire was for the purpose of instructing him. Job seems to get the point: he compares himself to dust and ashes, a symbol of human frailty and finitude.[7]

 FAITH ALIVE

Job believes himself to be a "brother of jackals" and a "companion of ostriches" (Job 30:30). Jackals are always mentioned in Scripture in reference to the wilderness except for one occurrence in Isaiah 43:20. Here, Isaiah speaks of a time when the desert will be transformed into a beautiful garden, and the jackals will praise the Lord. Ostriches are also associated with the wild, lonely places of the desert.

The irony in Job's language is evident when we read the speeches of God in Job 38—41 where many wild animals are described as wonders of creation, including the ostrich! Job was exactly where he needed to be—in the wilderness—in order for God to reveal to him a different understanding of security and blessing. He just doesn't realize that he is about to laugh with the ostriches (Job 39:18) and praise God with the jackals (Is. 43:20).[8]

Recall those "wilderness" times in your life when you were praying and thinking one thing, and all the while, God was preparing something extraordinary for you.

What are some things you have learned in the "wilderness"?

OATHS OF INNOCENCE

Job becomes specific about his integrity, proclaiming several oaths of innocence before God. As mentioned above, in the Bible, an oath is a self-curse announced by the speaker to assure that his words are true. From the following verses in chapter 31, list the oaths of Job:

Verses 1–6

Verses 7–12

Verses 13–23

Verses 24–28

Verses 29, 30

Verses 31, 32

Verses 38–40

How does Job "sign" the oaths? (vv. 35–37)

Do you believe these oaths are presumptuous, or are they a witness to Job's integrity?

 FAITH ALIVE

Impurity may result from a failure to make a commitment to moral purity. Commit yourself to moral purity. Keep your eyes, hands, and body pure from sin.[9]

It is always appropriate to renew specific disciplines in our lives. Job's oaths of innocence show how seriously he understood his moral behavior to be. List those godly activities in your life which God has helped you maintain.

Praise God for helping you remain morally pure.

1. Paul Lee Tan, *Encyclopedia of 7,700 Illustrations: Signs of the Times* (Rockville, Md.: Assurance Publishers, 1979), 618.

2. *Spirit-Filled Life® Bible* (Nashville: Thomas Nelson Publishers, 1991), 733, note on Job 28:1–28.

3. *Theological Wordbook of the Old Testament,* Vol. I (Chicago: Moody Press, 1980), 282–283.

4. J. Gerald Janzen, *Job* (Interpretation Commentary, Atlanta: John Knox Press, 1985), 191.

5. *Spirit–Filled Life® Bible,* 734, note on Job 29:1—31:40.

6. Ibid., 924, "Word Wealth: Prov. 31:28, blessed."

7. Janzen, *Job,* 208.

8. Ibid., 209, 210.

9. *Spirit-Filled Life® Bible,* 749, "Truth-in-Action through Job."

Lesson 6/Elihu's Challenge
Job 32—37

No one knew him. He set up his tent on the edge of town one Friday morning and by Saturday night had drawn a capacity crowd. Day after day he advertised his meetings with colorful flyers that promised miracles and words from God. Soon everyone was talking about the amazing man of God. Some claimed he could disclose the sins of a complete stranger and predict the future of anyone. He quoted beautiful passages from the Bible and seemed to defend God with great zeal.

Yet the evangelist's miracles and teachings soon began to be questioned. Did that man's right leg really grow another inch to match the left one? Was that woman really dying of cancer before she claimed to be healed? Was the evangelist's new teaching about prosperity completely biblical? Some felt his attitude had become presumptuous and overbearing.

After a couple of weeks, the tent was dismantled, and no one has heard from the man since. Was his ministry true? Was he really speaking for God? Some believed and some doubted. Perhaps that's the way it will always be.

THE DISCIPLINE OF GOD

Chapter 32 of Job introduces a new character in the story. Elihu was younger than Job's other three friends (Job 32:4), and in deference to their age, he waits until now to speak.

Why is Elihu's wrath aroused? (32:2–4)

Why do you think Elihu begins with such a long introduction? (32:6—33:7)

How does Elihu respond to Job's three friends? (32:6–12)

WORD WEALTH

Spirit (Job 33:4), *ruach* (*roo*-ach); Strong's #7307: Spirit, wind, breath. This word occurs nearly 400 times. In Genesis 6:17, "the *ruach* of life" is translated "the breath of life." Generally *ruach* is translated "spirit," whether concerning the human spirit, a distressing spirit (1 Sam. 16:23), or the Spirit of God. The Holy Spirit is especially revealed in Isaiah: God puts His Spirit upon the Messiah (42:1); He will pour out His Spirit upon Israel's descendants (44:3); both Yahweh and His Spirit send the Anointed One (48:16, a reference to the triune God); the Spirit of God commissions and empowers the Messiah (61:1–3).[1] The Book of Joel promises that the Spirit of God will be poured out upon all flesh (Joel 2:28).

The question arises as to the place of Elihu's speeches in the Book of Job. One way that Elihu challenges Job is in his claim to speak for God. In what ways does Elihu claim to have divine inspiration? (32:8, 18; 33:4. Also compare 32:19, 20 with Jer. 20:9.)

How do the following passages in Job challenge Elihu's claim to inspiration?

Elihu's anger toward Job (32:2–5) compared to God's lack of anger (Job 1:8–11; 2:3–6)

Job's words to his friends (26:4 and 27:3, 4)

The lack of any mention of Elihu in God's speeches (Job 38—41)

The lack of any mention of Elihu in the conclusion (Job 42:7–17)

 FAITH ALIVE

Just because someone claims to speak for God and uses all the "right words" doesn't mean that everything he says comes from God. Sometimes someone may think he is speaking for God, when he is really speaking for himself (i.e., Elihu). At other times, a person may think he is speaking only his own thoughts, when he is really speaking for God (i.e., Job). This is why discernment is so important in the church today.

How can the church distinguish between true and false claims to divine inspiration?

What are some practical ways the church can affirm true prophets of God, while still being careful of false ministers?

In what way does Elihu attempt to make Job comfortable with his speech? (33:1–7)

Describe the two ways in which God may choose to speak to people according to the following verses in chapter 33:

Verses 14–18

Verses 19–22

 PROBING THE DEPTHS

Elihu expands on the view of Eliphaz in Job 5:17–27 and points out that God may use suffering to instruct as well as to punish (33:19–30). According to one reading of the Book of Job, it is now possible to accept Job's testimony and still honor God as One who does right.[2] On the other hand, Job has already refuted Eliphaz' earlier speech (ch. 6) and claimed that he has done nothing which requires God's corrective actions. While God certainly can use suffering to chasten people, not all suffering is for that purpose.

Describe a time when you felt that God had allowed a difficult situation to remain in your life in order to instruct or chasten you.

What specific lesson did you learn?

How much was God directly involved in the process?

The Justice of God

In the second speech of Elihu (Job 34—35), the major theme is God's justice. In Job 34:5–9, what danger does Elihu describe of which Job should be aware?

 PROBING THE DEPTHS

Elihu does rebuke Job. He claims that calling God unfair is hardly a valid solution to the problem of suffering (34:10)! Twin themes dominate Elihu's discourse. The physical universe demonstrates that God's wisdom and understanding far surpasses humankind's. Why then should we expect to understand His ways of working in human lives? Since we are confident that God's character is marked by an abundant righteousness (see 37:23), when we cannot understand His actions we are simply to trust Him.[3]

In what way had Job come to this realization?

With what error does Elihu specifically charge Job? (34:35–37)

Although Elihu claimed to answer Job without using the "words" of Job's three friends (see Job 32:14), what similarities with the three friends do you see in Elihu's accusation?

 KINGDOM EXTRA

God's Spirit at Work. Elihu, in his debate with Job, makes three significant statements about the role of the Holy Spirit in His relationship to the people of God.

- The Spirit is the Author of wisdom (32:8). The Spirit endows one with the capacity to know and make sense out of life. Thus knowledge and wisdom are the Spirit's gifts to humankind.

- The Spirit is the Source of life (33:4). Apart from the direct influence of the Spirit, humanity as we know it would not have come into existence. From the original creation it was so and continues to be so.
- The Spirit is the Sustainer of life (34:14, 15). If God should turn His attention away from creation, if He should withdraw His life-giving Spirit from this world, then human history would end. Because He cares for us, God constantly sustains us by the abundant flow of His Spirit.[4]

Elihu continues his discourse (35:1–8) by noting that humans are affected by what they do, either for good or evil. Yet, he says that God is not affected by what humans do (vv. 6, 7). Eliphaz claimed the same thing when he said that God gained nothing from Job's righteousness (22:2–4). This was seen to be false, as the words of God and Satan make clear. Review Job 1:8–12; 2:3–6. What does God gain from Job's integrity?

In a similar way, in Job 35:9–13, Elihu claims that a person's cry to God should not be associated with the notion that God would be so intimate with humans as to "give songs in the night" (v. 10). In Elihu's view, such an attitude would be presumptuous. Yet, both Scripture and the experience of countless believers refute Elihu's view (see Ps. 32:7 and Acts 16:25).

Recount a time in your life when God gave you a "song in the night."

PROBING THE DEPTHS

Some theological traditions emphasize God's omnipotence to the exclusion of humankind's free will. In this view, nothing a person does affects God. He is the "unmoved Mover." The Book of Job, however, teaches that God *is* moved by the actions and the suffering of humans. God is sovereign, but His sovereignty allows for human choices which cause God sorrow or delight.

Name two or three human attitudes or actions which cause God sorrow.

Name two or three human attitudes or actions which cause God delight.

THE GREATNESS OF GOD

In Job 36—37, Elihu concludes his discourse with several statements "on God's behalf" (36:2). As was seen in chapters 32—35, Elihu's claim to divine inspiration is questionable, and his claim to speak differently from the three friends is false. Elihu's argument continues with the theme of God's omnipotence.

How might Elihu be said to be presumptuous? (36:3, 4)

To what extent does Elihu's teaching in Job 36:5–15 sound like the "retribution theology" of Eliphaz? (See 4:7–11.)

According to Elihu, why is Job still suffering the "judgment due the wicked"? (36:16–21) Is this assessment true?

According to the following topics, describe how Elihu develops the theme of God's greatness.

God's unapproachable rulership (Job 36:24–33)

God's greatness revealed in nature (Job 37:1–13)

God's incomprehensible power (Job 37:14–24)

Go back and read Job 9:2–13. Compare Job's statements in chapter 9 about God's greatness with Elihu's. If Job had answered Elihu at this point, what do you think he would have said?

How does Elihu's description of God's majesty in creation set the stage for God's speeches in chapters 38—41?

WORD WEALTH

breath (Job 37:10), *neshamah* (ne-sha-*mah*); Strong's #5397: Breath, breath of life, breathing person, living soul. This word first appears in Genesis 2:7, where God breathed into Adam's nostrils the *nishmat chayim*, "breath of life," and Adam became a living being. This is the tender account of how the first human took his first breath, aided entirely by the Creator, who shared His own breath with him. God literally taught humanity how to breathe.[5] Job emphasizes the dependence of all living beings on the sustaining breath of God. If it were to be removed, humanity would return to dust (Job 34:14, 15). In Job 37:10, nature is also sustained by God's breath.

 ## PROBING THE DEPTHS

In Job 36:1—37:24, Elihu emphasizes God's awesome power in order to establish that no one is ever justified in disputing Him. He appeals to nature as proof of God's power and wisdom. His summons to Job is, "Fear Him" (37:24).[6]

1. *Spirit-Filled Life® Bible* (Nashville: Thomas Nelson Publishers, 1991), 474, "Word Wealth: 2 Sam. 23:2, Spirit."
2. *Hayford's Bible Handbook* (Nashville: Thomas Nelson Publishers, 1995), 134, note on Job 32:1—37:24.
3. Ibid.
4. Ibid., 129, "Power Key: God's Spirit at Work."
5. *Spirit-Filled Life® Bible*, 879, "Word Wealth: Psalm 150:6, breath."
6. Ibid., 740, note on Job 36:1—37:24.

Lesson 7/God's Challenge
Job 38—42

No other experience on earth can take the place of being in God's presence. When our praise to God gets lost in inexpressible worship, when our questions dissolve and problems fade away as His Spirit sweeps over us and caresses our spirits, when we are confronted by the total Otherness of God, yet invited to participate in sweet communion—that is when we know God. Sometimes it is like a gently blowing breeze, and at other times it is like a whirlwind. We "see" God with our own "eyes" as Job did (Job 42:1–6), and we are changed.

Encounters with God also leave us with different understandings of the world and of ourselves. Whether we have interpreted our lives through the lens of long-held traditions or private notions, God often breaks those images and brings us into the freedom for which we were created—to be persons created in the image of God.

GOD'S WILD KINGDOM

God enters the drama with the final word. His response is not what we expect. He answers Job's questions with questions of His own. In a very real sense, He answers Job's questions with His presence.

Compare the ending of Job (chs. 38—41) with the ending of Habakkuk (see Hab. 3:3–15). Describe how both endings are similar.

PROBING THE DEPTHS

The arguments of the four men are all silenced by the voice of God answering out of the whirlwind. God challenges Job by comparing His omnipotence with Job's seeming impotence. He does this by describing the greatness of the earth (38:1–18), the complexity of the heavens (38:19–38), and His awesome design of the creatures of the earth (38:39—39:30). God then directly challenges Job to answer Him (40:1, 2).[1]

What is God's very first question to Job? (38:2)

In what way is this a rhetorical question?

In what way is this a genuine question which God expects Job to answer?

By calling Job "one who darkens counsel," (38:2) how does God refute Job's previous understanding of God's counsel or purpose for creation as recorded in Job 12:13, 22?

Instead of debasing Job, what does God challenge Job to do in 38:3?

PROBING THE DEPTHS

The series of questions God asks Job are important in revealing to Job (and to us) what kind of world God created. The first question to Job (Who are you?) is to be answered in the light of the kind of world in which *God shows Job to be,* not the kind of world in which *Job has perceived himself to be.* This is why the revelation of God is necessary for our human identity. It is significant that God did not tell Job directly who he (Job) is. Job must be involved in answering the question of who he is. This is the special place humans have as creatures who are made in the image of God.

According to the following topics, describe the *kind* of world God created. For each topic, write down how each element of creation is unmanaged or "wild" and how it is managed or "tame."

foundations (38:4–7)

sea (38:8–11)

morning/night (38:12–15)

underworld (38:16–18)

light and darkness (38:19–21)

weather and constellations (38:22–38)

animal life (38:39—39:30)

What one-word descriptions would you give to creation as it is presented here?

God concludes His first speech by asking Job if he can correct or instruct Him (Job 40:2). Like God's initial question (38:2), this question may also be taken as a genuine challenge to Job to lead him to a deeper understanding of his relationship to God.

PROBING THE DEPTHS

God describes creation as a world in which "wild" things exist, yet they exist within the bounds God has set for them (e.g., the sea). This comes through clearly in the discussion of the animals which are described as "wild," yet are governed by instincts given them by God. Why does God describe these things in this way to Job? One interpretation is to view all the questions asked of Job as God's way of "putting Job in his place" or debasing and humbling him. Such a view makes much of what Job has said in the dialogues false, and calls into question Job's belief in his own integrity. It also views God as siding with much of what Job's three friends have said about retributive justice, which is obviously not true according to God's rebuke of them in 42:7.

Another way to view God's questions to Job is to view them in the light of the primary question to Job, "Who are you?" In other words, who does God want Job to see himself to be (38:2) in the light of this description of creation? If God does not subscribe to the friends' view of retributive justice nor to Job's view of justice overturned, how should Job conceive of God's justice which is built into *this kind of creation?* Can Job truly instruct God? That is the question which is raised by this description of creation and with which Job struggles as he makes his first answer to God.

Job's first answer (40:4, 5) may be taken two ways. The first line of verse 4 may be translated "*Behold,* I am vile." This would mean that Job now sees himself to be a sinner who needs to repent, as his friends saw him all along. This view is called into question by God's rebuke of Job's friends in 42:7.

Another way to translate the first line of Job 40:4 is "If I am vile. . . ."[2] This would mean that Job realizes that if God wanted him to acknowledge that he was indeed vile, he has no basis on which to answer God (even though God commanded Job to answer Him). Job therefore chooses to remain silent. He has not yet decided how to answer God.

When is silence before God better than speaking?

WORD WEALTH

majestic (Job 39:20), *hod (hoad);* Strong's #1935: Glory, honor, majesty, beauty, grandeur, excellence in form and appearance. Appearing in twenty-four Old Testament references, *hod* refers to whatever or whoever is royally glorious. The word "splendor" may best define *hod.*[3] Here, the splendor of the horse is recounted as a wonder of God's creative power.

God's questions to Job have turned all the "why" questions into "who" and "where" questions. What does this shift reveal about how we try to attribute meaning to logic rather than to relationships?

BIBLE EXTRA

Compare the response of Job (40:3–5) with the experience of Isaiah who, when confronted with the holiness of God, sees himself as totally sinful and unable to stand before God (Is. 6). When he comes face-to-face with God, Job also comes face-to-face with his own self-understanding. Stripped of all he had and confronted by God's creative freedom, he sees himself as "without knowledge" and expresses his shame.[4]

Describe a time in your life when you were overwhelmed with the "otherness" of God. How did your response compare with Job's?

BEYOND HUMAN BOUNDARIES

God was not satisfied with Job's silence and begins another speech (40:6—41:34) which begins much like the first one, with a call for Job to answer Him.

In 40:6–14 God refutes Job's notion of God's justice. Review the following passages in the Book of Job and briefly describe how Job previously viewed God's justice

12:13–25

19:7

21:7–16

24:1–25

27:2

Of what does God accuse Job in 40:8? In what way is it a reversal of Job's accusation of God in 27:2?

Much of the message of the Book of Job turns on the question presented in Job 40:8: Can Job uphold God's justice and still claim his own innocence? In the light of the entire story, it is clear that both are true. What is being challenged here is not Job's innocence but his understanding of justice. God continues this challenge with a series of "do-it-if-you-can" imperatives in 40:9–14.

Review above how you described Job's understanding of justice. How do God's commands in 40:9–14 show Job's view of justice to be inadequate?

BEHIND THE SCENES

God compares Job's view of justice with certain creatures of the earth. The creature which is called "behemoth" (Job 40:15–24) may be a reference to the hippopotamus, and the creature called the "Leviathan" (Job 41:1–34) is perhaps the crocodile. Leviathan is used in Psalm 74:14 to refer to a mythic monster of the sea and in Ezekiel 29:3 as a symbol of the oppressive rulers of Egypt.

Read Job 41 and count the number of questions to which a negative answer is implied. Record your answer (   ).

In the remainder of His final speech (40:15—41:34), God confronts Job with two creatures which are beyond his comprehension to match in strength and majesty. What is God's point here? A clue comes in the final verse (41:34) where Leviathan is called "the king over all the children of pride." Job has already been challenged in 40:12 to "look on everyone who is proud and bring him low." God has presented two examples of proud creatures who cannot be "brought low," either by Job or by anyone else. In other words, Job needs another view of justice if he thinks that all the chaos in the world should and even can be done away with. God rules the world in a much different way, and the world God rules is much different than Job had imagined!

The following chart will help you compare the perspectives of Job, his three friends, and God.

	WHAT FRIENDS SAID	WHAT JOB SAID	WHAT GOD SAID
CREATION	total order	total chaos	both order and chaos
JUSTICE	strict retribution	indeterminate	creative/ redemptive
HUMANITY	sinners/ worms	dust and ashes	made in God's image to be co-rulers of the earth and participants in redemptive justice
GOD	Unmoved Judge	Prankster? Redeemer?	Creator/ Owner of a free and vulnerable world

    FAITH ALIVE

Our experience of nature puts us in touch with the transcendent aspect of God's creation. The mystery and majesty of creation should serve to keep us humble and thankful before the Creator.

For the next several days, make a list of things you observe in nature which reveal the mystery and glory of God's power. Include in your list things which seem "unmanageable."

Describe a time in your life when God broke through your perspective and brought new insight.

How can the church facilitate worship experiences which lead to the kind of encounter with God which Job had?

Job's second response to God (42:2–4) reveals that he repented or "changed his mind" about how he viewed the world, justice, humanity, and God.

In response to God's question "Who is this who hides counsel without knowledge?" how does Job describe himself? (v. 3)

In response to God's imperative for Job to listen to Him, how does Job respond? (v. 5)

In response to God's imperative for Job to answer Him, how does Job respond? (v. 6)

 ### PROBING THE DEPTHS

Job's repentance in 40:6 can be interpreted in different ways. Some understand that Job was repenting of sin and resigning himself to dust and ashes. If this is the case, then much of what the friends of Job had said was true. In Job 42:7, however, God rebukes the friends for not speaking the truth.

The repentance of Job can also refer to his change of mind concerning (Heb. *'al*) dust and ashes.[5] In this case, Job is "repenting" of the way he had defined himself and God in terms of the conventional theology of retribution. When confronted with calamity, this false view had led him to despise life and count humanity as worthless "dust and ashes" (see Job 30:19). He now changes the way he defines "dust and ashes" (i.e., humanity) to see them as God sees them, creatures who are made in the image of God and called to participate in the ordering of God's creation. This view also makes the most sense of God's affirmation of Job's words in Job 42:7.

JOB'S RESTORATION

The story of Job ends with scenes of reconciliation and restoration. What did God decide about the counsel of Job's friends? (42:7–10)

What do God's actions in allowing Job's friends to be "redeemed" say about the kind of justice God follows?

If God were following the kind of justice that Job's friends espoused, what might God have done to them?

In praying for his friends, how does Job fulfill Eliphaz' promise to Job in Job 22:26–30?

PROBING THE DEPTHS

God is more tolerant of Job's faith searching for answers than the three friends had been. God clearly states that what the three friends had said about Him was wrong, but He is silent in regard to Elihu. God neither affirms, acknowledges, rebukes, nor responds to him.[6] Although God had dialogue with Satan at the beginning of the story, He is now silent concerning Satan as well.

What theme in the Book of Job is underscored by God's silence concerning Elihu and Satan?

WORD WEALTH

prayed (Job 42:10), *palal* (pah-*lahl*); Strong's #6419: To pray, entreat, intercede, make supplication. *Palal* emphasizes prayer as intercession, asking someone with more power and wisdom to intervene in behalf of the one praying. For example, Hannah prayed for a son (1 Sam. 1:12); Hezekiah prayed for an extension of his life (Is. 32:2, 3); and Jonah prayed from within the fish's belly (Jon. 2:1–9). *Palal* is found in the promise of 2 Chr. 7:14, "If My people . . . will humble themselves, and pray . . . I will hear from heaven." Other examples of intercession include Genesis 20:7, 17; Numbers 11:2; and 1 Samuel 12:23.[7]

Job's restoration (Job 42:10–17) is described in ways which highlight the freedom of God's redemptive grace. List all the things which were given to Job.

verse 11

verse 12

verse 13

verse 16

What is striking about the naming of Job's daughters and not his sons? (vv. 13, 15)

What is striking about the daughters of Job receiving an inheritance along with their brothers? (v. 15)

What kind of justice is enacted by Job in naming his daughters and giving them an inheritance?

BIBLE EXTRA

In the Scriptures, restoration goes beyond the conventional understanding of "returning to an original condition." Job's experience of restoration illustrates that when God restores something, it is always increased or multiplied. What are the similarities in the following passages concerning restoration?

Joel 2:21–26

Exodus 22:1

Mark 10:29, 30

    ## KINGDOM EXTRA

Job's Affliction and Total Recovery (Job 42:10–13). Some point to Job to prove that sickness is God's will for many people. It is true that God permitted Job's illness to show Satan that Job would not turn from his Lord in the face of adversity. However, it is important to see that the affliction was a direct work of the devil (2:2). Further, illness was only one of Job's adversities. When God later healed him and restored all his losses two times over, the Hebrew text literally refers to his recovery as a return from captivity, an evidence that all his restoration was a driving back of evil, a recovering of something that had been "captured from him" (42:10).

Before we philosophize about "God's will" in sicknesses, we would be wise to note how God corrected Job's friends who had argued that his afflictions were a judgment from God (42:7–9). But Job's spirit of forgiveness toward his friends became pivotal for his own well-being and for theirs.[8]

FAITH ALIVE

Steps to Knowing God and His Ways. Knowing that God has sovereign freedom as Creator and Sustainer of the universe in both its physical and spiritual aspects must govern the way we think and behave. God is intimately involved in our lives in a way that eludes our grasp yet encourages us to participate in loving fellowship. Any wisdom that leads to truth comes from Him. The only way any person can know God is by specific revelation through personal encounter. Understanding God's true nature will lead us to a hope in redemption and eternal life.

Know and understand God as the Creator and Sustainer of the universe. Learn that He, not you, determines what is right.[9]

1. *Spirit-Filled Life® Bible* (Nashville: Thomas Nelson Publishers, 1991), 742, note on Job 38:1—42:6.

2. J. Gerald Janzen, *Job* (Interpretation Commentary, Atlanta: John Knox Press, 1985), 243.

3. *Spirit-Filled Life® Bible*, 606, "Word Wealth: 1 Chr. 29:11, majesty."

4. Ibid., 745, note on Job 40:3–5.

5. Janzen, *Job*, 255–256.

6. *Spirit-Filled Life® Bible*, 746, 747, note on Job 42:7–9.

7. Ibid., 747, "Word Wealth: Job 42:10, prayed."

8. Ibid., "Kingdom Dynamics: Job 42:10–13."

9. Ibid., 748, "Truth-in-Action through Job."

EXPLORING THE DEPTHS OF LIFE'S MEANING
ECCLESIASTES 1—12

It is human nature to ask questions. We were created to investigate and inquire in order to learn. Many of us, however, never get around to asking the ultimate questions about life. We often keep questions about the meaning of life well hidden behind present occupations or future dreams.

Ecclesiastes peels back the cloaks of apathy and denial and asks some very blunt yet necessary questions. Until we face the realities of human limitations, we will continue to deceive ourselves that we can save ourselves. Ecclesiastes makes us painfully aware of this. Its primary message is, "Without God, life is utterly meaningless."

Lesson 8/The Human Quest for Meaning
Ecclesiastes 1—2

We all like to get new things. We learned this early as children who always wanted the newest toy. Of course we would play with it for awhile, but most of the time, it would eventually end up in the back of the toy box or in the closet as we discovered yet another new toy. And so the cycle continues in adulthood. We buy new clothes, new cars, new homes, always looking for something else as the new wears off. In reality there really isn't anything "new" when it comes to material possessions. Even technology has become boring as "new" gadgets take up more and more space in our lives. It seems that nothing in this life truly satisfies. A recent popular phrase captures the idea well. We say we've "been there, done that." We are left with the question, "Does anything in life have permanent value?"

This is exactly the subject taken up by the author of Ecclesiastes hundreds of years ago. As he says, "There is nothing new under the sun."

WHO WAS THE PREACHER?

The Book of Ecclesiastes is unique in the Bible, as a quick reading will show. At first glance it seems depressing and very human-centered. And it is! At least most of it is. In order to understand Ecclesiastes, it is helpful to think like a secular person, to set aside your belief in God and all that is revealed in the New Testament about Jesus Christ, and to imagine what human life would be like without God. Think of this book as a dark backdrop to allow the good news of the gospel to shine forth even more brightly.

What are your thoughts about the Book of Ecclesiastes which you have gathered through the years?

As you read the first section (Eccl. 1:2–11), what is your initial reaction?

BEHIND THE SCENES

Ecclesiastes is generally credited to Solomon (about 971 to 931 B.C.), written in his old age. The rather pessimistic tone that pervades the book would be in keeping with Solomon's spiritual state at the time (see 1 Kin. 11). Although not mentioned in 1 Kings, Solomon must have come to his senses before his death, repented, and turned back to God. Ecclesiastes 1:1, "The words of the Preacher, the son of David, king in Jerusalem," seems to point to Solomon. Scattered throughout the book are allusions to Solomon's wisdom (1:16), wealth (2:8), servants (2:7), pleasures (2:3), and building activities (2:4–6).[1]

Some biblical scholars assign the book to a later date and claim that the author ascribes the book to Solomon to borrow his authority. In this case, the book is a critique of the meaning and purpose of life in words Solomon might have used.

BEHIND THE SCENES

The name *Ecclesiastes* is derived from the Greek word *ekklesia* ("assembly") and means "One Who Addresses an Assembly." The Hebrew word so represented is *qoheleth,* which means "One Who Convenes an Assembly," thus often being rendered "Teacher" or "Preacher" in English versions.[2]

Some scholars translate the Hebrew word for "Preacher" *(Qoheleth)* as "Professor," indicating the academic nature of the book and the "wisdom tradition" from which it came. In fact, it may be helpful to imagine the "Professor" in his classroom with his students, and the curriculum is whatever may be observed about life. This "Professor" takes up the viewpoint about life which we today would call secular humanism. He does not adopt this viewpoint as the final word, but he investigates the limits of this viewpoint and reaches conclusions which are fully biblical, as we will see.[3]

What role should secular education play in society today?

What role should secular and religious education play in the life of the believer and in the church?

SEARCHING FOR PERMANENT VALUE

The Preacher begins the report of his investigation (Eccl. 1:2–11) with a summary of his findings. From the human vantage point, he has found that everything is utterly meaningless. What a way to start a book in the Bible! At least he has our attention. Name some things in life which you would describe as "meaningless."

 WORD WEALTH

"Vanity" is a key word in the book, translating the Hebrew *hebel* (literally, "breath"), thus indicating what is mortal, transitory, and of no permanence. As the Preacher tries each of the avenues proposed by humanity to achieve the value sought, he finds them elusive ("grasping for the wind") and fleeting, transitory ("vanity"). The Hebrew word translated "profit" is *yitron* (1:3), and may also be translated "gain, value."[4]

PROBING THE DEPTHS

> The question posed in verse 3 is the true theme of the book. What gives genuine value or advantage *(yitron)* to existence? Can that factor be found in the present life? The question posed by the Preacher explains why everything is useless: there is no gain, no profit, no abiding value to humankind from labor in this life.[5]

As you read this opening section (1:2–11), list all the things associated with the idea of "sameness."

List the "cycles" named in this section.

What human emotion is shown most clearly in this section?

How does Ecclesiastes 1:11 describe life as an eternal now?

From the message in this introductory poem, what answer to the question posed in verse 3 do you think the Preacher is leaning toward?

What does the Preacher believe about "human progress"?

To what extent does secular life today match the Preacher's description and analysis?

How would you challenge the findings of the Preacher if you could talk with him in person?

Attempted Solutions

Having given the reader (or "students") his initial report, the Preacher now begins a review of his investigation (Eccl. 1:12—2:26). What biographical information may be learned about the Preacher from Ecclesiastes 1:12–15?

How did the Preacher go about his investigation?

What was the scope or extent of the investigation?

What resources were at the Preacher's disposal?

What was the Preacher's initial conclusion? (v. 14)

Restate verse 15 in your own words. (Here's your chance to write a proverb!)

What particular things might the Preacher have in mind as "crooked" or "lacking"? (v. 15)

There are three major areas of investigation discussed in the next section: wisdom (1:16–18; 2:12–16); pleasure (2:1–11); and work (2:17–26).
What was the Preacher's view of his own wisdom? (1:16)

Was his method "academic" or "practical"? (1:17)

What was his initial conclusion concerning the gaining of wisdom? (1:17, 18)

WORD WEALTH

The pursuit to know "madness and folly" in addition to "wisdom" (Eccl. 1:17) should be understood in the light of the practice within the wisdom tradition of dividing humanity into the categories of "wise" or "foolish" for the purpose of giving straightforward advice (as in the Book of Proverbs). The Preacher claims to have "known" (i.e., personally experienced) both wisdom and folly so that his investigation would be as thorough as possible.

The Preacher reaches other conclusions about wisdom and folly in Ecclesiastes 2:12–16. In his opinion, which is best, wisdom or folly? (v. 13)

What is the "same event" which happens to both the wise and the foolish? (v. 14)

How does the Preacher express his frustration about the futility of wisdom? (v. 15)

What is the Preacher's understanding about death? (v. 16)

FAITH ALIVE

The death of a close friend or family member often becomes an occasion when we reevaluate our perceptions of death and consider our own death. When we experience the loss of a loved one, our sense of security is put to the test. Our frailty is exposed.

In what way do you think that the Preacher's perception of death is universal?

Do you avoid thinking about death? If so, why?

What difference does a Christian understanding of death make for the Preacher's conclusion?

The next pursuit of the Preacher is pleasure (Eccl. 2:1–11). List the specific ways in which he indulged his sense of pleasure (vv. 3–8).

What was the extent of his pursuit of pleasure? (v. 10)

What positive reward does pleasure give? (v. 10)

What is his conclusion concerning the lasting value of pleasure? (v. 11)

 WORD WEALTH

special (Eccl. 2:8), *segullah* (seh-goo-lah); Strong's #5459: Possession, personal property, special treasure. Of the eight times this noun is used in the Old Testament, five references speak of Israel as God's special treasure. Two passages, including Ecclesiastes 2:8, speak of the prized possessions of kings, or "royal treasures." The remaining reference is Malachi 3:17, which speaks of the people whom God will regard as His "jewels." While humans consider material possessions as special treasure, God's treasure is human beings.[6]

The final area of investigation made by the Preacher is work (Eccl. 2:17–26). Why did the Preacher hate his labor? (v. 18, 19)

In verse 21, the Preacher gives an example of someone who has the highest qualifications. An example of such a person today would be a highly trained scientist or doctor. What is upsetting the Preacher about this sort of person's labor?

To what degree do you sympathize with the emotional state of the Preacher presented in verse 20?

Summarize how the Preacher describes human labor. (vv. 22, 23) To what extent do you agree or disagree with this description?

What is the Preacher's conclusion concerning labor? (v. 23)

[book icon]   **BIBLE EXTRA**

The Preacher acknowledges (Eccl. 2:24, 25) that he cannot take the fruit of his labor beyond this life. If he cannot take it with him and is uncertain as to how his heirs would treat it, one should enjoy what one has while he is alive. Enjoyment of what one has as a blessing from God is an important secondary theme of the book; it will reappear frequently.[7]

Trace the development of the theme of enjoyment of God's blessings in the Book of Ecclesiastes through the following references:

2:20–25

3:10, 11, 22

5:11–15

5:18–20

6:1, 2, 9

9:7–12

 FAITH ALIVE

Although they do not hold the permanent value the Preacher is searching for, enjoying the blessings of the Lord in this life still gives us a sense of personal and familial comfort. What are some ways in which you consciously enjoy your work?

List your favorite foods. Give thanks to the Lord for them!

What other nonreligious activities and events do you enjoy?

Plan an outing to your favorite restaurant this week.

1. *Spirit–Filled Life® Bible* (Nashville: Thomas Nelson Publishers, 1991), 927, "Ecclesiastes: Introduction, Author and Date."
2. Ibid.
3. Kenneth O. Gangel, *Thus Spake Qoheleth: A Study Based on an Exposition of Ecclesiastes* (Camp Hill, Penn.: Christian Publications, Inc., 1983), 10.
4. *Spirit-Filled Life® Bible*, 928, "Ecclesiastes: Introduction, Content."
5. Ibid., 931, note on Ecclesiastes 1:3.
6. Ibid., 288, "Word Wealth: Deut. 26:18, special."
7. Ibid., 933, note on Ecclesiastes 2:24, 25.

Lesson 9/*Empty Ways*
Ecclesiastes 3—6

Gaius Aurelius Valerius Diocletianus (better known as Diocletian) was emperor of the Roman Empire from A.D. 284 to 305. He had come to power rather quickly, advancing through the ranks of governor, consul, and finally commander of the palace guards. Upon his inauguration as emperor, he promptly organized the empire so that a line of successors to the throne was set in place in succeeding positions, from second-in-command to third and fourth.

After twenty years of ruling, however, Diocletian became bored with his power and tired of the endless pressures which came with such a lofty position. In his twenty-first year, he yielded his reign to Maximian who begged him to remain. Diocletian had made up his mind, however, and remarked to Maximian that the pursuit of power would not be so tempting even to Maximian if he could see the cabbages which Diocletian had cultivated with his own hands at Salona.[1]

Positions of authority do not guarantee happiness or fulfillment. In fact they often produce disappointment and boredom, or at the least, burnout. Ecclesiastes speaks to such issues with blunt realism. Life is often better lived in a garden raising cabbages.

CHANGING THE TIMES

In one of the best-remembered passages from Ecclesiastes (3:1–8), the Preacher recounts a list of activities in which people may be engaged. The highly rhythmic literary style of this list reminds us of the never-ending tick-tock of a clock or the mesmerizing swing-swing of a pendulum as we read, "A time to. . . . A time to. . . . A time to. . . . A time to. . . ."

How does this poem relate to the earlier conclusions of the Preacher? (Eccl. 1:9)

Comment on the saying, "Variety is the spice of life." Does the Preacher agree with this saying?

From this list, which events do we not have any control over?

What pair(s) of activities would you add to this list?

WORD WEALTH

times (Eccl. 3:1), *'et (eht);* Strong's #6256: A particular time; season, age, occasion, or some period of time; current times. Unlike *'olam,* which refers to a vast expanse of time, *'et* is used to describe a small space of time. *'Et* can be a season, such as Passover season, rainy season, or harvest season (see 2 Chr. 35:17; Jer. 51:33; Zech. 10:1). It may refer to a portion of a lifetime, "time of old age" (Ps. 71:9).[2] The meaning of *'et* is well illustrated in the present passage. There is an "occasion" for everything that happens.

Review the story of creation in Genesis 1 and compare it with Ecclesiastes 3:1–8. In what ways are these two passages similar?

PROBING THE DEPTHS

Humanity, in attempting to change the cycles of nature (creation), is actually attempting to change the order God has established. But this is not a power allotted to humankind, and God will call persons into account for their actions.[3]

What are some recent evidences of the breakdown of the intended order in creation caused by human domination of nature?

What does Ecclesiastes 3:9–12 reveal about God and God's plan for human existence?

Is there a legitimate joy in life for those who do not know God? (3:12, 13)

What does Ecclesiastes 3:14, 15 reveal about God and time?

To what extent should we think of time as our possession to be spent? (3:14, 15)

What limit or boundary encloses human activities within time? (3:11, 15)

What two attitudes toward God should human beings exhibit according to verses 13 and 14?

Compare the thoughts of Ecclesiastes 1:9 and 3:15. Write down each saying using the words, "past," "present," and "future."

 FAITH ALIVE

Developing Humility. One message in Ecclesiastes comes through loud and clear: Walk gently and humbly before the Lord. "God is in heaven, and you on earth." The more we know about God, the more humble we will be. The humble person recognizes his own limitations and accepts them.

Accept and recognize that human understanding is partial and distorted. Know that the facts humankind has forgotten could change your perspective entirely.

Accept your limitations. Know that you cannot comprehend eternity. Learn to accept God's perfect timing. Understand that the pursuit of personal ambition is vain and futile.[4]

PERVERTING JUSTICE

The Preacher now moves into the public arena of life and discusses the relationships people have and the injustices which abound there (Eccl. 3:16—4:16).

Describe the injustice caused by the wicked. (Eccl. 3:16, 17)

What solution does the Preacher offer in this situation? (3:17)

The Preacher's understanding that humans and animals share the same destiny (death) troubles him because justice is cut short by death. What questions still remain in his mind concerning life after death? (3:21, 22)

What is the Preacher's conclusion regarding how the righteous should live? (3:22)

When the Preacher observed the oppressed, what brought him distress? (4:1–8)

In the light of the oppression which abounds, who is "best off"? (4:3)

According to the Preacher, in what ways do those who are alone have to cope with more problems? (4:7–12)

List the ways in which "two is better than one." (4:9–12)

Why is youth favorable to old age? What injustice is described here? (4:13–16)

According to the Preacher, does merely having a position of authority guarantee you honor at the end of your life? (4:16)

WORD WEALTH

Judgment (Eccl. 3:16) is translated from the word *mishpat* which appears around 400 times in the Old Testament. *Mishpat* refers to the totality of governmental functions including judicial, executive, and legislative aspects. It is best defined by the word "justice." *Mishpat* finds its source in God and cannot be separated from His person (Deut. 1:17). It refers to the right ordering of life under God's sovereignty. The Law and ordinances of God are just because they correspond to the character of God.[5] In this passage the preacher laments that justice has been overrun by wickedness.

BIBLE EXTRA

In Ecclesiastes 4:1–3 the Preacher considers those in the world who suffer oppression. In a statement brimming with passion, he finds the oppressed have no comforter (champion), and power lies on the side of their oppressors. Because of these two factors, the oppressed have no hope. Death seems better than life.[6]

Reflect on the following passages in the light of the Preacher's conclusion. How does Ecclesiastes differ from other responses to injustice recorded in Scripture?

Deuteronomy 15:7–11

Psalm 74:21

Isaiah 5:7–17

Amos 4:1–5

James 2:1–9

WORSHIP AND WEALTH

The Preacher's attention turns now to religion and wealth (Eccl. 5:1–12). From the passage about worship (5:1–7), describe the way the Preacher contrasts listening and speaking.

List the ways in which this passage (5:1–7) calls us to be serious about worship.

Summarize the Preacher's definition of a religious "fool" from this passage (5:1, 3, 4).

What connection do you see between words, dreams, and vows? (5:2–7)

FAITH ALIVE

Taming the Tongue (Eccl. 5:1–7). When we speak, we must be aware that the Lord hears every word we say. Presumptuous speech displeases the Lord and can bring discipline.

Be quick to listen and slow to speak. Cultivate humility and learn to walk softly before the Lord. Do not speak presumptuously of spiritual commitment or endeavor. Cultivate reverence for the Lord.[7]

An undisciplined tongue can get you into deep trouble. Keep a list throughout the week of things you wish you hadn't said. Review your list to see if there is a pattern of associated subjects. Ask the Holy Spirit to help you overcome this habit.

 BIBLE EXTRA

The Holy Spirit at Work. All references to "spirit" in Ecclesiastes are to the life-force that animates the human or the animal (see 3:18–21). The book nevertheless anticipates some of the problems faced by the apostle Paul in the implementation of spiritual gifts in 1 Corinthians 12—14. People who believe that God speaks to them through the Holy Spirit in dreams and visions (Joel 2:18–32; Acts 2:17–21) would do well to heed the wise advice of the Preacher that not every dream is the voice of God (Eccl. 5:3).

In what way is this advice similar to the admonition of Paul in 1 Corinthians 14:29?

How does the Preacher's stress on reverence and obedience parallel Paul's concern for the edification of the church (1 Cor. 14:5)?[8]

The Preacher turns his attention next to money (Eccl. 5:10–12). According to Ecclesiastes 5:10, what is the danger inherent in gaining wealth?

What two problems will wealthy persons always have according to the Preacher? (Eccl. 5:11, 12)

List some examples from today's society which illustrate the point of Ecclesiastes 5:11.

    FAITH ALIVE

Handling Money. Being a righteous steward of worldly wealth flows out of a godly perspective with regard to money. Money is a servant to utilize, not a god to serve. One's motives in acquiring and using money are the determining factors.

Consider and understand that wealth is intrinsically elusive. Understand that wealth is by its very nature deceptive. Know the difference between wealth that has been sought and wealth that has come from the hand of God.[9]

Make a list of the things which you possess or services you require in your lifestyle which you have to pay to maintain. How many of these are "necessary"?

In what ways do we "serve" the things we own?

If you have lost sleep over material possessions (see Eccl. 5:12), ask the Lord to direct your steps to reduce your possessions so that you may live healthier and without stress.

LIFE'S DISAPPOINTMENTS

The Preacher has a way of peeling back the wrappings and getting to the realities of life, harsh as they may be. In this section (Eccl. 5:13—6:12) he points out that much of life is a fraud.

How can riches hurt their owner? (5:13)

In what ways are material possessions not secure? (5:13–17)

Is there permanent value in having riches? (5:16)

In the light of the insecurity of material possessions, what attitude and action does the Preacher recommend? (5:18–20)

 ### FAITH ALIVE

The Preacher has taken great pains to explain how wealth cannot bring lasting satisfaction. Yet, there is joy in this life. Read Ecclesiastes 5:20 and list the "joys of your heart."

If you have become preoccupied with obtaining material things which only add stress to your life, ask God to keep you busy with the joys of your heart.

According to the following topics, summarize why many good things in life are insecure and potentially unsatisfying.

Wealth (6:1, 2)

Children (6:3–6)

Long life (6:3–6)

Work (6:7–9)

Being human (6:10–12)

 PROBING THE DEPTHS

Wealth and material gain do not and cannot satisfy (Eccl. 5:10). All human systems of economics, whether Marxist, socialist, or capitalist, are predicated on materialism, and thus are futile.[10]

In what ways does the consumer mentality of American culture tempt believers?

What practical steps can be taken to avoid falling into the trap of trusting in economic security to satisfy spiritual needs?

How can Christians instill in the next generation a biblical value system?

FAITH ALIVE

What advantage is there to one's spiritual well-being in acknowledging human limitations?

In what ways have you become disappointed with life?

Identify any steps you need to take to recover your satisfaction with the gifts God has given you to enjoy.

1. Paul Lee Tan, *Encyclopedia of 7,700 Illustrations: Signs of the Times* (Rockville, Md.: Assurance Publishers, 1979), 217.

2. *Spirit-Filled Life® Bible* (Nashville: Thomas Nelson Publishers, 1991), 1003, "Word Wealth: Is. 33:6, times."

3. Ibid., 934, note on Ecclesiastes 3:14, 15.

4. Ibid., 944, "Truth-in-Action through Ecclesiastes."

5. *Theological Wordbook of the Old Testament,* Vol II (Chicago: Moody Press, 1980), 948, 949.

6. *Spirit-Filled Life® Bible,* 934, note on Ecclesiastes 4:1.

7. Ibid., 945, "Truth-in-Action through Ecclesiastes."

8. Ibid., 929, 930, "Ecclesiastes: Introduction, The Holy Spirit at Work."

9. Ibid., 945, "Truth-in-Action through Ecclesiastes."

10. Ibid., 936, note on Ecclesiastes 5:10.

Lesson 10/The Limits of Human Wisdom
Ecclesiastes 7—10

Back in the days when ocean-going vessels were powered by wind and sail, the most feared area in the sea was the doldrums. The doldrums are regions in the ocean near the equator which are characterized by calms, squalls, and light, baffling winds. Ships caught in the doldrums could wait for days or even weeks for the wind to blow enough for them to continue their journey. The weather was often hot and stifling, causing discontent and depression among the crew members.

Being "in the doldrums" has become an expression for people who seem to be caught in a state of inactivity, boredom, and melancholy. They may be very busy people, but they feel stuck in an endless cycle of monotonous activity. Time seems to drag on and on with relentless regularity. The Book of Ecclesiastes portrays life as a doldrums-like experience. Chapters 7—10 are focused especially on "how to live in the doldrums." The point is that since we are caught in this windless sea, why not make the most of it? Let's face up to reality and deal with things as mature persons.

MAKING THE MOST OF IT

At first glance, Ecclesiastes 7 seems to be a list of several proverbs which support the theme of enjoying what God has given (see Eccl. 5:18–20). After all, wisdom is better than foolishness, even if wisdom is relative. Upon closer inspection, however, the proverbs paint a bitterly realistic picture of life within the limits of human understanding. If people must limit their potential to this earthly life, this is the best they can hope for.

In each pair of contrasts noted from chapter 7, which reality is better according to the Preacher? What reason(s) does he give for his choices? Do you agree or disagree? Why?

Reputation or wealth? (v. 1)

Death or birth? (v. 1)

Mourning or feasting? (v. 2)

Sorrow or laughter? (v. 3)

Rebuke or praise? (v. 5)

The end or the beginning? (v. 8)

Patience or pride? (v. 9)

 FAITH ALIVE

Look back through the list above. According to today's society, which of each pair is valued more. Be honest!

In what ways do we as a society avoid thinking about death and sorrow?

What is the benefit of considering death?

In some of the contrasts, the Preacher sounds extremely pessimistic. What role, if any, do you think pessimism should play in the believer's life?

To what does the Preacher compare wisdom in verses 11, 12? Which is of greater value? Why?

In verse 13, the Preacher presents his basic understanding of reality. What does this verse tell us about God?

About reality?

About human limitation?

In the light of Ecclesiastes 7:29, are humans included in what God made "crooked"?

What limit does the Preacher acknowledge for human life in verse 14?

How does the biblical teaching about prayer change this limitation?

To what extent does the Preacher's method of investigation (i.e., empirical observation) affect his conclusion?

 BEHIND THE SCENES

Ecclesiastes 7:15 is a critique of the conventional theology of retribution, which the Book of Job also powerfully challenges. The Preacher's observation contradicts the notion

that the righteous will always live long and prosperously while the wicked will be judged quickly. This observation is the basis for his advice to avoid extremes.

List the extremes one should avoid, according to verses 15–18. What reasons are given for avoiding these extremes?

What attitude can keep a person from living in extremes? (v. 18)

What limitation does the Preacher identify concerning the "just person"? (v. 20)

Why should we not trust everything people say about us? (vv. 21, 22)

Write down your reaction to verse 22.

WORD WEALTH

Cursed (Eccl. 7:22) is translated from *qalal* (kah-*lahl*) which has the basic meaning of "to make light of someone" or "to ridicule another person." In its adjective form, it means "easy, trifling; having very little weight." For examples of its use in reference to matters that are considered "light," or of relatively small weight, see 1 Kings 12:9; 2 Kings 20:10; and Isaiah 49:6. Examples of its use as "curse" or "make light of someone" include Genesis 12:3; 2 Samuel 16:13; and Ezekiel 22:7.[1] In the present reference, the Preacher acknowledges the human inclination to make light of others.

Describe the limits of wisdom according to verses 23, 24.

What human experiences did the Preacher seek to know? (v. 25. see also 1:17; 2:12)

 PROBING THE DEPTHS

In his search for wisdom, folly, and madness, the Preacher explains that he found the woman who entraps to be even more bitter than death (Eccl. 7:25, 26). It is likely that the reference here to "woman" should be taken figuratively.

The immediate context supports the interpretation that an *untimely death* is more bitter than death. In this view, the conventional wisdom of retribution theology kicks in to explain verse 25: the sinner is cut down quickly (cf. Eccl. 7:15).

The wisdom tradition also offers the interpretation of the entrapping woman as the opposite of wisdom, i.e., *folly*. This understanding is implied in Proverbs (chs. 4—5) with its contrast of the lady wisdom and the seducing woman.

What does the Preacher say in verses 27, 28 about finding trustworthy people? To what extent do you agree or disagree?

What is the one thing the Preacher is sure about? (v. 29)

How far does the insight of verse 29 go to explain much of what causes the Preacher distress?

COPING WITH LIFE'S PERPLEXITY

As we get older, we realize that life really is quite perplexing at times. We can deny the problems of life and live as pre-pain people, but we will never reach maturity that way. The Preacher calls us to face the hard challenges of life. To grow in wisdom is to deepen our character.

Divide chapter 8 into three sections according to the topics of authority, crime, and injustice. List your divisions.

According to verses 2–5, how should one approach authority?

What cannot be controlled by an earthly king? (v. 8)

Give current examples of the Preacher's critique of power in verse 9.

What observation had the Preacher made concerning delayed punishment of crime? (vv. 10, 11)

In what way do verses 12 and 13 agree and/or disagree with Ecclesiastes 7:15?

According to verses 12 and 13, does the Preacher support or reject the traditional teaching of retribution theology?

How does verse 14 challenge the traditional teaching of retribution theology?

According to verse 15, what is the best way to cope with life's difficulties?

What limitation does wisdom have? (vv. 16, 17)

FAITH ALIVE

Dealing with Sin (Eccl. 8:8, 11). The wise person understands that to willfully practice sin is to become its slave, and to delay in dealing with sin appropriately is to promote it.

Understand that you are the slave of any wickedness that you practice (see Rom. 6:16). Carry out any discipline you determine is necessary without delay, because delay may foster wrongdoing.[2]

Chapter 9 of Ecclesiastes is perhaps the most pessimistic. The perspective offered here reaches the outer limits of secular human meaning. The bottom line is that there is nothing secure in this life. What does the Preacher say about the following topics?

Destiny (9:1, 2)

Death (9:3–6)

Human desires (9:7–10)

Chance (9:11, 12)

Contempt (9:13–18)

WORD WEALTH

grave (Eccl. 9:10), *she'ol* (sheh-*oal*); Strong's #7585: The grave; the abode of the dead; the netherworld; hell. This noun occurs sixty-five times, its use broad enough to include the visible grave that houses a dead body and the abyss, that unseen world to which the soul departs in death. The meaning of "grave" is seen in Genesis 37:35; 42:38; and 1 Kings 2:6. *She'ol* speaks of the realm of the departed souls in such verses as Psalm 9:17; 16:10; 55:15; 139:8; Isaiah 14:9–11; and Ezekiel 31:15–17; 32:21. The assumed root of *she'ol* is *sha'al,* "to ask, demand, require." Thus "hell" is a hungry, greedy devourer of humanity, is never full or satisfied, but is always asking for more (see Proverbs 27:20).[3] The present verse highlights the finality of death for those whose hope is limited to this earthly life.

PROBING THE DEPTHS

The generally skeptical tone of Ecclesiastes stands in contrast to the Book of Proverbs, where an optimistic confidence assumes that life is fundamentally logical and consistent, with wise choices producing good results and foolish choices producing bad results. Ecclesiastes recognizes that this is frequently not the case. Here Ecclesiastes does not simply contradict Proverbs, but supplements it with a different but equally necessary perspective. There are inexplicable mysteries about life which defy easy solutions.[4]

FAITH ALIVE

In leaving certain difficult problems unsolved, Ecclesiastes poses profound questions regarding the meaning and coherence of life—questions that can only ultimately be answered in Jesus Christ, for only Christ can provide ultimate satisfaction, joy, and wisdom.[5]

What problem or issue, personal or societal, causes you to want to give up?

Ask the Holy Spirit to illuminate your understanding and comfort your heart as you face this problem.

AVOIDING FOOLISHNESS

The theme of chapter 10 is foolishness. If wisdom is desirable (even with its limitations), foolishness should be rejected outright. The thought here is that if one is to live within the confines of human understanding, then at the least, avoid being a fool!

What are some "dead flies" which might cause the kind of problems mentioned in verse 1?

According to verses 2 and 3, how is folly revealed?

Name some practical examples of the wonderful advice in verse 4.

What "evil" is named in verses 5–7?

  BEHIND THE SCENES

Ecclesiastes 10:2 distinguishes the right hand and the left hand in terms of good and evil. In the ancient world the right symbolized good fortune and the left symbolized bad fortune.

List the ways of the foolish person described in verses 8–15. Which of these examples do you observe in your own surroundings?

According to the following topics, describe the ways in which foolish actions can be detrimental to human life.

Immaturity (vv. 16, 17)

Laziness (v. 18)

Indulgence (v. 19)

Gossip (v. 20)

BEHIND THE SCENES

Money answers everything (Eccl. 10:19). The Preacher has just stated the purpose for the feast (laughter) and wine (makes merry). Money, on the other hand, can be spent or invested, and the one who has it always retains options that are automatically forfeited by the person who has spent all his cash.[6]

FAITH ALIVE

Keep a journal of your daily activities for several weeks. Review these activities weekly and place each activity under the general categories of wise or foolish. (Be self-critical here!)

Reflect on the benefits of a wise lifestyle. Seek to live by the wisdom God gives you for the tasks at hand (James 1:5).

1. *Spirit-Filled Life® Bible* (Nashville: Thomas Nelson Publishers, 1991), 1070, "Word Wealth: Jer. 8:11, slightly."

2. Ibid., 945, "Truth-in-Action through Ecclesiastes."

3. Ibid., 1272, "Word Wealth: Hos. 13:14, grave."

4. *Nelson's Complete Book of Bible Maps and Charts: Old and New Testaments* (Nashville: Thomas Nelson Publishers, 1993), 190, 192.

5. Ibid.

6. *Spirit-Filled Life® Bible*, 941, note on Ecclesiastes 10:19.

Lesson 11/Conclusion: Fear God
Ecclesiastes 11:1—12:14

The young woman was startled when she opened the box of roses to find that most of the petals were falling off and the leaves were wilting. The flowers were from her next door neighbor, an elderly woman who was always doing nice things for her. Thinking that perhaps the florist was delayed in delivering the roses, she thanked the kindly old woman the next chance she had. When her neighbor told her that she had cut them several days ago and had been enjoying their beauty and fragrance, the young woman looked puzzled. Her neighbor explained that she had sent the wilting flowers to her as an object lesson. The neighborly lady had overheard the young woman say that she had no intentions of living for God while she was young, but would become a Christian after she had enjoyed life for a while. The gift of wilting roses was meant to show her what she was doing to the Lord by waiting. The young woman took the lesson to heart and soon became an exuberant follower of Jesus Christ.[1]

The conclusion to the Book of Ecclesiastes is a call to both the young and the old to fear the Lord. The Preacher's message is, "Do not wait until the rose petals are wilted and lifeless. Give your life to God now."

HOPE FOR THE FUTURE

The Preacher moves into a more positive stance in chapter 11 of Ecclesiastes. The insecurity of life opens up the possibility of success as well as failure. In the light of these possibilities, the Preacher advises that it is okay to take some risks. Describe the attitude of the Preacher toward the following topics:

Investment (11:1, 2)

Risk (11:3, 4)

Anticipation (11:5, 6)

According to the following categories, what specific activities might be included in the Preacher's daring advice in 11:1–6?

Financial

Spiritual

Personal

WORD WEALTH

prosper (Eccl. 11:6), *chashar* (kah-*shar*); Strong's #3787: To be right, successful, proper, correct; to be correctly aligned with certain requirements. *Chashar* occurs three times in the Old Testament: in this reference; in 10:10, "bring success"; and in Esther 8:5, where the queen presents her request on condition that it "seem right" to the king. *Chashar* thus describes whatever is right, fitting, and proper; furthermore, something will prosper and be successful simply because of its "rightness." Its postbiblical derivative *kosher* means that food is properly prepared according to Jewish dietary laws derived from Scripture and rabbinic specifications.[2]

What connection does the Preacher make between giving and being prosperous?

How does this passage (11:1–6) relate to Jesus' words in John 9:4?

FAITH ALIVE

While the Bible never makes the claim that giving to God's purposes yields automatic returns on money, the Scriptures do encourage an attitude of openness and generosity which should characterize the believer. These attitudes are encouraged because they are elements of God's character. It is God's nature to bless His children.

Make a list of ministries or charitable organizations to which you already give or could add to your contributions in the future.

Support these ministries with prayer and ask God to direct you in giving financially to each one.

JOYFULNESS FOR THE PRESENT

The Preacher finds it in himself finally to say, "Look on the bright side" (11:7–10). Although all that is coming is vanity, joy is still a present possibility. Yet, a long life of joyful bliss is also vanity.

According to the following topics, describe the advice of the Preacher recorded in Ecclesiastes 11:7, 8.

Pleasure?

Balance?

Death?

What might the "light" of verse 7 represent?

From where does this light ultimately come?

How does this point to the book's final conclusion? (12:13)

According to the following topics, describe the counsel the Preacher gives to the young (11:9, 10):

Pleasure

Tension

Judgment

 PROBING THE DEPTHS

In Ecclesiastes 11:7–10 the entire mood of the book changes and the first summary of the conclusion occurs. The Preacher has failed to find anything of lasting value "under the sun" (in this life), since life itself is transitory and impermanent. Thus he is driven to two conclusions:

- In this life the best thing to do is to enjoy the blessings of God (see also 5:18–20).
- Any absolute value must transcend this life, finding itself rooted in the justice of God (11:9). Knowing that God will judge all things should motivate us to lead moral lives (11:10) even in the course of enjoying the things with which He has blessed us.[3]

 FAITH ALIVE

Make a list of the things in your life which bring you joy.

Leave this list in a conspicuous place to remind you throughout the day to give thanks to God for His blessings in your life.

GODLINESS IN YOUTH AND OLD AGE

In another well-remembered passage from Ecclesiastes (Eccl. 12:1), the Preacher begins a reflection on the nature of youth and aging. What metaphors are given for the process of growing older?

Ecclesiastes 12:1, 2

Ecclesiastes 12:3, 4

Ecclesiastes 12:5

 WORD WEALTH

Remember (Eccl. 12:1), *zachar* (zah-*char*); Strong's #2142: To remember, bring into mind, recollect; also, to mention, meditate upon, mark down, record, recall, and retain in one's thoughts. To remember something or someone is to approve of, to acknowledge, and to treat as a matter of importance, whereas to forget something or someone is to dismiss or abandon as unimportant. God remembered Noah, Abraham, Rachel, and His covenant (Gen. 8:1; 19:29; 30:22; Ex. 2:24). In the new covenant, God promises to never again remember Israel's sin (Jer. 31:34). In the present reference, the young are called to live in relationship with God before the difficulties of life harden the heart.[4]

 FAITH ALIVE

Knowing God and His Ways (Eccl. 12:1). We are to revere God as the Creator who works everything perfectly after the counsel of His own will.

Believe that everything God does is perfect. Establish your relationship with God while you are still young, before the evils of life harden your heart.[5]

According to Ecclesiastes 12:7, what happens to a person's spirit at death? How does Paul advance the teaching of Ecclesiastes in 1 Corinthians 15?

The Preacher's closing words (Eccl. 12:8) are almost identical to his opening report (Eccl. 1:2). This device forms a literary envelope into which the author has placed his observations about the futility of secular human life. Compare your initial reactions to the statement, "All is meaningless," as you read Ecclesiastes 1:2 with your feelings about the same statement here at the conclusion of the book. How are they different?

FAITH ALIVE

How old were you when you became a believer in Christ?

What regrets, if any, do you have about not coming to the Lord sooner?

What advice would you give an adolescent or teenager who has not made a commitment to serve God?

OBEDIENCE FOR ETERNITY

Ecclesiastes 12:9–14 is a concluding commentary on the Preacher's life and teachings, probably written by a student of the author. From this summary, describe the influence of the Preacher on those around him.

How does this fact affect the way we read and reflect on the Book of Ecclesiastes?

How did the Preacher affect the lives of others?

In what ways are the words of the Preacher in Ecclesiastes like nails? (12:11)

What is the conclusion of the Preacher's observations? (12:13, 14)

How does the fear of God change our outlook on life?

The following chart helps illustrate how the Preacher shows the difference between the vanity of godless living and the fulfillment which comes as a result of godly fear.

Without God "all is vanity":
Godless learning ⟶ cynicism (1:7, 8)
Godless greatness ⟶ sorrow (1:16–18)
Godless pleasure ⟶ disappointment (2:1, 2)
Godless labor ⟶ hatred of life (2:17)
Godless philosophy ⟶ emptiness (3:1–9)
Godless eternity ⟶ unfulfillment (3:11)
Godless life ⟶ depression (4:2, 3)
Godless religion ⟶ dread (5:7)
Godless wealth ⟶ trouble (5:12)
Godless existence ⟶ frustration (6:12)
Godless wisdom ⟶ despair (11:1–8)
The beginning of wisdom is the fear of God, a deeply serious attitude toward the commands of God.
GODLY FEAR ⟶ FULFILLMENT (12:13, 14)[6]

We are admonished to live in relationship to God and in the light of the future judgment of every deed (12:14). Review the statements of the Preacher in the following passages and discuss how this perspective might change the secular viewpoint which colored these earlier sections?

1:1–11

2:12–16

5:23–26

5:27–28

 PROBING THE DEPTHS

Ecclesiastes 12:9–14, like 1:1, 2 are written in the third person, showing the work of a disciple who arranged the book of the Preacher's work in its present form. The disciple wants the reader to understand the importance of his teacher's work (vv. 9–11), after which he adds a summary in his own words, probably quoting his teacher in verses 12–14, in order to make sure the reader really has understood the point being made.

Although the increase of books and human knowledge will never cease, human wisdom yields values that are limited and transitory and thus bring weariness. By contrast, reverence for God and the obedience that is its natural outgrowth are literally humanity's all, a term that stands in sharp contrast to the things of this world that are found to be "vanity." Those things will pass away, but one's relationship with God will stand at the time when He judges the earth (v. 14).

Was, then, the Preacher's quest futile? By no means. It showed clearly where one's priorities should lie; not in the things of this life, but in God.[7]

FAITH ALIVE

The Preacher counsels his readers toward godly living. We are to live with a view to the futility and vanity of a life spent without reference to God. Much of the energy we spend trying to accomplish various tasks ends up "sowing to the wind." The life lived in fidelity and integrity is the only one that has any real meaning.

Seek to please God in all you do. Conduct a Spirit-filled life. Serve the Lord with all your might. Cultivate the fear of the Lord.[8]

FAITH ALIVE

Wisdom from God. The author closes this book by stating that there is a God who will hold us accountable for the deeds of our lives. Life "under the sun" will be judged from a heavenly perspective. Thus the book ends on a positive and encouraging note, because one's accountability before God means that the course of one's life is of eternal significance.

In spite of frequent observation and experience of life's apparent futility, the author exhorts his readers to grasp by faith the sovereignty, goodness, and justice of God and to enjoy all the facets of life as His gift.[9]

What portion of the Book of Ecclesiastes spoke to you most forcefully? Why?

What commitment to the Lord is the Holy Spirit prompting you to make or renew after having studied Ecclesiastes?

1. Richard W. De Haan, *The Art of Staying Off Dead-end Streets* (Wheaton, Ill.: Victor Books, 1974), 148, 149.

2. *Spirit–Filled Life® Bible* (Nashville: Thomas Nelson Publishers, 1991), 942, "Word Wealth: Eccl. 11:6, prosper."

3. Ibid., note on Ecclesiastes 11:7–10.

4. Ibid., 1044, "Word Wealth, Is. 62:6, make mention."

5. Ibid., 944, "Truth-in-Action through Ecclesiastes."

6. *Nelson's Complete Book of Bible Maps and Charts: Old and New Testaments* (Nashville: Thomas Nelson Publishers, 1993), 192.

7. *Spirit-Filled Life® Bible*, 943, note on Ecclesiastes 12:9–14.

8. Ibid., 944, "Truth-in-Action through Ecclesiastes."

9. *Nelson's Complete Book of Bible Maps and Charts: Old and New Testaments*, 191.

EXPLORING THE DEPTHS OF LOVE
SONG OF SOLOMON 1—8

Everyone loves the magic and mystery of a wedding. The anticipation builds as plans are made, invitations are sent out, flowers and candles are put into place, and family and friends are gathered together. Finally the big moment arrives. The couple is joined together as husband and wife. Irrepressible smiles spread among those gathered as they witness the mystery of the union of a man and woman before a holy God. Tears of joy express mixed feelings of fear and hope for a life-long journey of love and fulfillment. So it is today, so it has always been.

From the Garden of Eden to the garden of love in the Song of Songs and even until today, marriage has as its attendants longing and joy, desire and contentment. The Song of Solomon is perhaps the best description of married love ever written. It tempts us with its playful words. It invites us in like witnesses at a wedding. Like a tapestry, it now hides, now reveals as it weaves the story of the love of a man and woman from anticipation to fulfillment and contentment.

Lesson 12/The Quest for Authentic Intimacy
Song 1—8

Walk into almost any bookstore today and you will see an entire section devoted to "romance novels." Most of these stories are cheap fantasies, conjured up in the imaginations of writers whose primary purpose is to feed the twisted cravings of love-starved and lust-filled readers. These fantasies indeed stir up passion, but they also portray love as a manipulative game or obsessive fixation, where adultery and fornication are justified with the label, "mutual consent."

Such deceptive stories are a far cry from the true love and authentic intimacy God desires a man and a woman to share within the protective bonds of covenant commitment.

The Song of Solomon offers its readers a story of authentic love. The Song abounds with images of mutual giving and receiving, of intimate moments and exciting anticipation, of endearing words spoken within the context of a supportive community in which vows of love are taken seriously. Above all it expresses the joy of God in creating humankind as male and female.

ANTICIPATION

When a couple becomes engaged, there is nothing more exciting than the anticipation of marriage. In the Song of Solomon, the story of love between the bride and groom begins (1:1—2:7) with mutual expressions of desire, self-doubt, and joyful expectation as they anticipate their future together. The Song of Solomon reads like a play or script with alternating speakers. As you witness their journey, it is important to notice who is speaking in the text (see NKJV insertions).

If you are married, share with your spouse memories of your engagement and the anticipation of your wedding day.

BEHIND THE SCENES

Solomon's authorship is disputed, but the glory of Solomonic symbolism is essential to the Song. Jesus referred twice to Solomon's glory and wisdom (see Matt. 6:29; 12:42). As David's royal son, Solomon had a unique place in covenant history (see 2 Sam. 7:12, 13). His two birth names, which symbolize peace (Solomon) and love (Jedidiah), readily apply to the Song (2 Sam. 12:24, 25; 1 Chr. 22:9).

Solomon's glorious kingdom was like a restoration of the Garden of Eden (1 Kin. 4:20–34), and the temple and palace he built embody the truths of the tabernacle and the conquest of the Promised Land (1 Kin. 6:7). Solomon is perfectly cast as the personified blessings of covenant love since he appears in the Song with all of his regal perfection (Song 1:2–4; 5:10–16).[1]

PROBING THE DEPTHS

The literary form and intent of the Song have been understood in a variety of ways which may be reduced to three basic approaches.

1. The *allegorical view* understands the book as a poem describing the relationship between God and Israel or between Christ and the church. Each detail is seen as symbolic of deeper spiritual truth.

2. The *typological view* differs from the allegorical by acknowledging the historical foundation and by finding analogy not in all subordinate details, but only in the main outlines. Proponents of this view acknowledge the mutual love between Solomon and the Shulamite, but go beyond that to consider the divine analogy with its more elevated and spiritual meaning as being the more important.

3. The *literal view* takes the content of the Song at face value. Some who interpret it that way maintain that the poem

is a secular love song expressing human romantic love at its best without spiritual lesson or theological content, but a literal interpretation need not mean that the book has no spiritual illustrations or application.[2]

BEHIND THE SCENES

The text of the Song of Solomon mentions fifteen geographical locations from Lebanon and Syria in the north to Egypt in the south. The term "Shulamite," identifying the king's lover, appears only in 6:13 and may be derived from the town of Shunem which was southwest of the Sea of Galilee in the tribal area of Issachar.

Locations in the Song of Solomon[3]

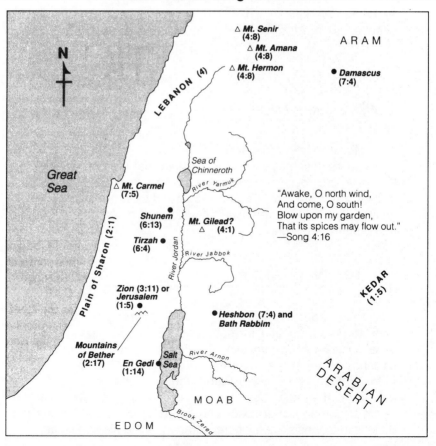

How does the bride express her anticipation of her wedding? (1:2, 3)

How does the groom express his affection for his wife-to-be? (1:8–10, 15)

What tension is expressed in 1:6? What possible problem could this cause for the marriage?

What is the role of the Daughters of Jerusalem? (1:4, 11) How can we as readers be compared to this group?

FAITH ALIVE

Moral Purity. Maintaining sexual purity until marriage is a key to establishing a strong Christian marriage. In view of the prevailing social acceptance of sexually immoral behavior, it is of great importance that God's holy people renounce impurity and make a renewed effort to rebuild commitment to moral purity in the church.[4]

WORD WEALTH

love (Song. 1:4), *'ahab* (ah-*hahv*); Strong's #157: To love, to have affection for someone; to like, to be a friend. *'Ahab* is remarkably similar to the English word "love" in that its range of meanings cover the same ideas. *'Ahab* can refer to loving God, loving one's friend, romantic love, love of ideals, love of pleasures, and so on. The participial form refers to a friend or spouse. The first mention of love in the Bible is in Genesis 22:2, where Abraham loved his son Isaac.[5]

FAITH ALIVE

Understand that physical desires for your spouse are entirely appropriate. Refuse any sexual involvement before marriage, knowing that it

1) diminishes sexual fulfillment within marriage

2) compromises necessary objectivity in important pre-marital evaluations and decisions

3) seriously weakens a couple's ability to make necessary sexual adjustments within marriage.[6]

PROBING THE DEPTHS

"Love" is the key word in the Song. This love, presenting the passionate desire between a man and a woman, King Solomon and the Shulamite, celebrates the joyous potential of marriage in light of sworn covenant principles. The basis for all human love should be covenant love, the master metaphor of the Bible.

This covenant love is also the basis of the relationship between God and humankind; therefore, the Song applies properly to both marriage and to covenant history. The Shulamite therefore personifies the wife in an ideal marriage and the covenant people and their history in the Promised Land under the blessings of royal Solomonic love.[7]

What emotion come through most clearly in this initial section (1:2—2:7)?

What evidence of the equal exchange of love is exhibited?

OPENNESS

The journey moves into the phase of courtship (Song 2:8—3:5) as the bride and groom exchange loving invitations to be with one another.

According to the following topics, how does the poem describe the elements of courtship?

Playfulness (2:8, 9)

Exclusiveness (2:10–14)

Admiration (2:27)

Desire (3:1–5)

FAITH ALIVE

Advice to Dating Couples. Using courtship to maximum advantage minimizes difficulties in marriage. Many couples enter marriage unprepared to deal with the things they will face. Though brief and indirect, the advice given by Solomon and the Shulamite should be heeded by those preparing for marriage.

Understand that it is of the utmost importance that we learn to know and accept our intended spouse as he or she is. Accept as wrong thinking any hidden plans to change that person. It is better not to follow through with plans for marriage than to marry one you cannot accept as he or she is.

Take time to identify and resolve potential problems to your marriage. Face them honestly and candidly. Determine to build a strong, unbreakable commitment to each other in your marriage.[8]

WORD WEALTH

stir up (Song 3:5), *'ur (oor);* Strong's #5782: To rouse, awaken, stir up, excite, raise up; to incite; to arouse to action; to open one's eyes. Occurring about seventy-five times in the

Old Testament, *'ur* is used of an eagle stirring up its nest (Deut. 32:11) and of a musical instrument being awakened or warmed up for playing (Ps. 108:2). In Isaiah 50:4, the Lord awakens the prophet each morning and "awakens" his ear to hear God's message. See also Isaiah 51:9, which speaks of the arm of the Lord being awakened or roused into action.[9] The present reference warns against beginning the process of loving exchange until the appropriate occasion and opportunity is present.

MUTUALITY

The wedding day has arrived! The royal wedding procession is described by the bride in Song of Solomon 3:6–11. What elements of the procession would you attribute to the fact that the groom was the king?

Who was the king's mother? (3:11)

What significance does the blessing of the king's mother have in the story?

Several elements of the procession reflect the story of the redemptive journey out of Egypt by the people of Israel. Look up the following passages and note the similarities.

The journey out of the wilderness (Exodus; Song 3:6)

The appearance of God's glory (Ex. 16:10–15; Song 3:6)

The pillar of cloud and fire (Ex. 13:21; 30:34–38; Song 3:6)

The wedding is described in a love poem written by the groom about his bride (4:1–7). Much of his description of her physical beauty is taken from the natural surroundings in Palestine. List the references to nature used in the description of the bride.

It is always appropriate to compliment those we love, affirming the beauty God has given them. Love is often renewed and kept alive by endearing yet simple words of affection. If you are married, describe your spouse in poetic terms. Use your imagination (like Solomon did!). Share your description with your spouse.

Weddings are followed by wedding nights! The story continues (Song 4:8—5:1) in an exchange of poems by the groom and bride as they tell of the rapture of sexual love. Once again, images of nature fill this section. List how the different physical senses are engaged in this description of love.

Smell

Touch

Taste

Sight

Hearing

What does this use of all the physical senses indicate about the goodness of the body and the appropriateness of physical love?

Compare and contrast the imagery of the woman as a fragrant garden with the imagery of the Garden of Eden in Genesis 2—3.

 BEHIND THE SCENES

The Holy Spirit at Work (Song 4:16). According to Romans 5:5, "the love of God has been poured out in our hearts by the Holy Spirit." On the basis of Jesus Christ, the Holy Spirit is the bond and the binding power of love. The joyous oneness revealed in the Song is inconceivable apart from the Holy Spirit. The very form of the book as song and symbol is especially adapted to the Spirit, for He Himself uses dreams, picture–language, and singing (see Acts 2:17; Eph. 5:18, 19).

A subtle wordplay based on the divine "breathing" of the breath of life (the Holy Spirit, see Ps. 104:29, 30) in Genesis 2:7 seems to surface in the Song. It shows up in the "break" or breathing of the day (Song 2:17; 4:6), in the "blowing" of the wind on the Shulamite's garden (4:16), and surprisingly in the fragrant scent and fruit of the apple tree (7:8).[10]

 FAITH ALIVE

Keys to an Enduring Marriage. Successful marriages result from the disciplined practices that have been proven through the centuries by countless couples whose love and commitment grew stronger and more passionate. Today when the cultural environment wars against the Christian marriage—seeking to redefine, dilute, and delude our understanding of God's institution—recovering these dynamic principles is essential.[11]

FAITH ALIVE

Marriage Partners. Learn the lost art of verbal lovemaking. Learn to speak words of love that caress your spouse's soul.

Understand and believe that the Lord continues to view the sexual relationship within the sanctity of marriage as "very good" and to bless it.[12]

Being true to life, the story is not without its tensions (Song 5:2–8). The bride spends the night alone and wonders why her husband has not returned to her. She seeks him, but does not find him. What attitude is displayed by the bride in this section?

How should we interpret her delay in opening the door? (5:3, 4)

ONENESS

Tensions melt as the husband and wife make up (Song 5:9—8:4). This section begins with a description of the husband by his wife (5:10–16). When asked where he has gone, her reply indicates that the king has a retinue of women whom he frequents (see 1 Kin. 11:3). His return is indicated by her acknowledgment in 6:3, "I am my beloved's, and he is mine."

It is now his turn to praise her beauty (6:4–10). In the context of his absence and return, what does this poem indicate about their relationship?

 WORD WEALTH

friend (Song 5:16), *re'a* (*ray*-ah); Strong's #7453: Friend, companion, neighbor, fellowman; a familiar person. This noun occurs more than 180 times. Its root is the verb *ra'ah*, "associate with," "be a friend of."[13] The present reference points to the mutuality and companionship enjoyed in marriage.

 FAITH ALIVE

Throughout your marriage extol your spouse's virtues above those of others. Set aside regular, periodic times away with your spouse to refresh and renew the romance in your marriage.[14]

The beloved answers the praises of her husband by comparing him to a garden (see 5:1) which is in full bloom. Note the mutuality of loving exchange in this poem.

 BEHIND THE SCENES

Solomon's ardent call to return (6:13) is given against the backdrop of the wandering of God's covenant people, a backdrop to which he alludes in his reference to Mahanaim, the two camps. Mahanaim is the memorial name of a supreme event in covenant history (Gen. 32). It marked the return of the national family to the land (see Gen. 32:9; Hos.

14:1). Here Jacob received his new name, "Israel," "Prince with God," God's name joined to Jacob's. Mahanaim magnified grace and truth by contrasting the unworthy smallness of Jacob in his departure from the land, with only a staff, with his massive fruitful return as two companies (see Gen. 32:9, 10; Amos 7:2, 5).[15]

Renewal of love is described in matching poems which praise the physical virtues of wife (7:1–9) and husband (7:9—8:3). List images from nature employed in these poems.

Comment on how the author both unashamedly reveals and yet delicately conceals with his tapestry of words.

FULFILLMENT

The story concludes with images of lasting fellowship and fulfillment (Song 8:5–14). Visiting relatives and sharing happy times among family members is a natural part of a fulfilling marriage. What does the mention of Solomon's mother imply in Song of Solomon 8:5?

The wife's brothers describe their young sister (8:8, 9). How does the wife relate their description to herself? (8:10)

 FAITH ALIVE

Christian parents should get involved in the development of your children's sexual morality. Encourage and support their sexual purity and virginity. Build defenses against attempts to seduce them away from sexual righteousness.

Value virginity very highly! Do not ever discredit the inestimable value of being able to present to your new spouse your body and soul, wholly undefiled and kept pure for him/her.[16]

Solomon is given a choice between the wealth of his vineyards or the different kind of wealth which his wife can bring to him (8:11, 12). How does this section describe the maturity of Solomon's wife?

WORD WEALTH

companion (Song 8:13), *chaber* (chah-*vehr*); Strong's #2270: A friend, companion, partner, associate; someone joined together or knit together with another person. *Chaber* comes from the verb *chabar,* "to join together, fellowship, associate with." In this reference, the plural *chaberim* refers to "friends" who are closely bonded together in love or in a common purpose.[17]

The love story ends with the wife's call to her husband to come and enjoy the pleasures of love.

BIBLE EXTRA

Christ Revealed. In the Song of Solomon, as in other parts of the Bible, the Garden of Eden, the Promised Land, the tabernacle with its ark of the covenant, the temple of Solomon, the new heavens and the new earth are all related to Jesus Christ, so it is not a matter of merely choosing a few verses that prophesy of Christ. The very essence of covenant history and covenant love is reproduced in Him.[18]

In the light of the following verses, how does the message of the Song of Solomon relate to Jesus Christ and our relationship with Him?

Luke 24:27

2 Corinthians 1:20

2 Timothy 3:15, 16

1. *Spirit-Filled Life® Bible* (Nashville: Thomas Nelson Publishers, 1991), 946, "Song of Solomon: Introduction, Author."

2. *Nelson's Complete Book of Bible Maps and Charts: Old and New Testaments* (Nashville: Thomas Nelson Publishers, 1993), 195.

3. Ibid., 196, 197.

4. *Spirit-Filled Life® Bible,* 956, "Truth-in-Action through Song of Solomon."

5. Ibid., 837, "Word Wealth: Ps. 97:10, love."

6. Ibid., 956, "Truth-in-Action through Song of Solomon."

7. Ibid., 957, "Truth-in-Action through Song of Solomon."

8. Ibid., 946, "Song of Solomon: Introduction, Purpose."

9. Ibid., 1359, "Word Wealth: Hag. 1:14, stirred."

10. Ibid., 947–948, "Song of Solomon: Introduction, The Holy Spirit at Work."

11. Ibid., 957, "Truth-in-Action through Song of Solomon."

12. Ibid.

13. Ibid., 906, "Word Wealth: Prov. 17:17, friend."

14. Ibid., 957, "Truth-in-Action through Song of Solomon."

15. Ibid., 954, note on Song of Solomon 6:13—7:9,"

16. Ibid., 956, "Truth-in-Action through Song of Solomon."

17. Ibid., 858, "Word Wealth: Ps. 119:63, companion."

18. Ibid., 947, "Song of Solomon: Introduction, Christ Revealed."

SPIRIT-FILLED LIFE® BIBLE DISCOVERY GUIDE SERIES

*Coming Soon

Spirit-Filled Life® Kingdom Dynamics Study Guides

Other Spirit-Filled Life® Study Resources

Spirit-Filled Life® Bible, available in several bindings and in NKJV and KJV.

Spirit-Filled Life® Bible for Students

Hayford's Bible Handbook 0-8407-8359-0